TOWARDS A CONSTITUTIONAL CHARTER FOR CANADA

T0326991

ALBERT S. ABEL

Towards a Constitutional Charter for Canada

UNIVERSITY OF TORONTO PRESS
Toronto Buffalo London

Reprinted from *University of Toronto Law Journal* 28, 3(1978)261–363

CONTENTS

TOWARDS A CONSTITUTIONAL CHARTER FOR CANADA

ALBERT ABEL'S CONSTITUTIONAL CHARTER FOR CANADA

*Introduction**

Albert Abel's death interrupted his work on devising a new constitution for Canada, and on the book in which he had begun setting out and elaborating his constitutional proposals. What follows is the first, largely completed, portion of that unfinished book.

The conception of the constitution which animated his proposals was far from unfinished or incomplete. As a critic of past constitutional interpretation, he had reproached the courts with ignoring what he saw as the organizing premise of the British North America Act's allocation of legislative power: that parliament should manage the national economy, while 'the patterns, values, and institutions of everyday community contact' should be the domain of the provinces.[1] It was this premise, rather than the judicial interpretation, which was in his view consistent with the distinctive features of Canada as a country – 'her geography and her diverse societies'[2] – and with the basic functions and responsibilities of government. What he had in mind for the future constitution was a fresh attempt to implement this premise, in an arrangement resembling the European Economic Community.[3] Haphazard drafting had misled the courts in the past;[4] by careful drafting, he would secure the new structure against the distortion which had been the fate of its predecessor.[5]

In an address to the Law Students' Society at the University of New Brunswick in 1976, entitled 'A Chart for a Charter,'[6] he outlined the core of his constitutional proposals, the new division of powers between parliament and the legislatures of the provinces.[7] As the replacement for section 91 of the BNA Act, he suggested the following:

* I am grateful to Larissa Tkachenko, a third-year student in the Faculty of Law, for her assistance in preparing this material for publication.
1 Abel, The neglected logic of 91 and 92, (1969), 19 *U.T.L.J.* 487, at 500–01
2 Abel, A chart for a charter, (1976), 25 *U.N.B.L.J.* 20, at 23; infra, at 270
3 A chart for a charter, supra note 2, at 29; infra, at 304
4 A chart for a charter, supra note 2, at 24–5; infra, at 271, 291
5 See infra, at 31–4.
6 Supra note 2
7 Ibid, at 25–6

Parliament may make laws as to[8]

1 The structure and functioning of the economy including but not limited to
A money
B credit institutions
C transportation and communication facilities and services of substantial significance to more than one province
D labour, capital, and commodity transactions having substantial effects on their respective markets in more than one province
E industrial and intellectual property.
2 Abuses of the natural environment having substantial consequences in more than one province.
3 External affairs including the enforcement of the provisions of treaties made under section ( ).
4 The raising of money by any mode or system of taxation.
5 Subject to the provisions of this Constitution, the organization and operations of the federal government.
6 Except as provided by section (   ), the public debt and property.
7 The government of areas within Canada lying outside the boundaries of any province and of the National Capital Territory as defined in Schedule (   ).
8 Defence against war or insurrection.

Two new provisions would complete parliament's array of powers:

The power to make treaties is federal. It is coextensive with the power of parliament to legislate under [the preceding] section.

Federal moneys may be used for carrying out laws in relation to the powers granted to or recognized in the federal government by section (   ) and otherwise only as directed by the Canadian Equalization Council[9] except with the unanimous concurrence of the provinces.

Section 92 would be replaced with this section:

Each provincial legislature may make laws operative within the province as to anything not assigned by Section (   ) to parliament. This power extends but is not limited to laws dealing with
1 The constitution of the province.
2 Municipal and local authorities.
3 The raising of money by any mode or system of taxation.

8 In 'A Chart for a Charter,' the phrase was 'parliament may make laws about ...' For reasons discussed infra, at 290–1, he later concluded that the wording which appears in the text would better confine federal power to its desired sphere.
9 In 'A Chart for a Charter,' the reference (apparently in error) was to 'the Canadian Economic Council.' The Canadian Equilization Council is proposed and discussed infra, at 338–63.

4 Civil and criminal law and procedure without prejudice to the power of parliament to provide for carrying out measures enacted in the exercise of powers given it by this constitution.

Finally, the relationship between federal and provincial laws would be specified as follows:

Federal laws are paramount except that as regards matters specified under subsection (1) paragraphs (c) and (d) and under subsection (2) of section (   ), if all relevant provinces have parallel provisions, the provincial law shall apply.

These were the proposals whose restatement and amplification Albert had begun in the manuscript of his book. In coming to them he drew upon a variety of sources. Australia and the United States are the conventional comparisons, but Albert's constitutional wisdom was never merely conventional; in the constitutions of Malaysia and Mexico he found models to emulate and to avoid. Ultimately, however, the proposals – and particularly his expression of them – were uniquely Albert Abel's.

Some explanation is warranted of the way in which his work was prepared for publication. The manuscript which he left comprised six chapters and the beginning of a seventh: General Principles and Primary Assumptions; an untitled chapter dealing with his allocation of the residuary power to the provinces; Taxation; Spending; The Canadian Equalization Fund and Council; Economic Regulation; and The Inflation and Deflation of Federal Competence (an historical account of the federal commerce power in Canada, Australia, and the United States).

The first five chapters are substantially reproduced below. The sixth and seventh, with an eighth chapter not begun, were to comprise a part of the book to be entitled 'The Canadian Common Market.' Since the sixth chapter was to be an introduction to the proposals elaborated in the eighth,[10] and since the seventh chapter was only barely begun, they are omitted. In the material which is reproduced, references to proposals left undeveloped are retained, as indications of the intended coverage of the constitutional charter.

Footnoting the manuscript posed a problem of some difficulty. Throughout the text were noted the places where footnotes were to be inserted, and, particularly in the first few chapters, many of the footnotes themselves were completed. But in other instances, sources were noted only cryptically or not at all. Accordingly, much of the preparation consisted of supplying appropriate references, which may be less ample than would ordinarily be expected. Occasionally, editor's notes of an explana-

10 The proposals themselves are set out supra, at 4, as subsection 1 of the section assigning powers to parliament.

tory nature were also required; in the material which follows, they are designated alphabetically to distinguish them from other footnotes.

Given the opportunity to introduce his own work, Albert might have repeated something which he said at the conclusion of his address to the New Brunswick law students:

There is no near prospect of anything like [these proposals] being accepted. There is an absolute certainty that something along these general lines will ultimately come to pass or Canada will dissolve. Self-preservation being as strong an instinct with politicians as with the rest of us, they will stagger along bantering patchwork solutions at each other. Even if agreement on that basis can be reached, anything short of a fundamental remodelling taking account of the needs and conditions of national life will not suffice. Those in authority will not discard familiar patterns until the very eve of a breakup. It may then be too late.

Like Noah, I seek to build an ark against the day when the flood comes. Unlike Noah, I do not expect to be around to use it. But others will.[11]

J.B.L.

11 A chart for a charter, supra note 2, at 53 (footnotes omitted).

1 GENERAL PRINCIPLES AND PRIMARY ASSUMPTIONS[a]

Assertion of one's own personality seems a primary desire of those formed in the western cultural tradition. We do not like to be told what we may or must do. Many, though, feel qualified, as having a mission even, to prescribe rules of conduct for others, not necessarily from a naked wish to bully but often in complacent confidence that applying their scale of values will promote the common good. Friction is inevitable.

Foregoing absolute individual autonomy is a cost of living together. Society entails accommodation. Therein lies the occasion for and the office of governments. Their great diversity illustrates the demand for being free to make one's own choice with the imperatives of a viable social structure.

The more heterogeneous a group, the smaller the element of concordant personal preferences. Increased size by itself brings a greater mix of attitudes concomitant to the greater population. The physical, material, and cultural milieus too are important; when similar they polarize individual inclinations, when dissimilar they diffract them. Since, by definition, large political units affect many people, it is to be expected that there will be present in them a wider array of geographical, historical, and economic factors. Control by them will collide with individual choices more extensively and probably more intensively than will that by more compact communities.

Clearly, though, a large unit has more resources and so more power than a small. Exertion of that power has been seen as appropriately a function of government. That is within limits valid. It conflicts, however, with the dislike of having to submit to the will of others. Nobody undertakes to justify erratic exercise of state power. To be respectable it must be purposive. There is never complete consensus on purposes but, by so far as government action falls short of it, by just that much it approaches tyranny.

Collective action can indeed operate to enlarge effectively as well as to curtail individual liberty. Without some minimum means available, individuals cannot achieve and at the extreme may cease to aspire to personal

a Portions of this chapter previously appeared in A chart for a charter, (1976), 25 *U.N.B. L.J.* 20.

realization beyond bare existence. Measures which create or preserve the conditions necessary to avoid that promote rather than diminish the aggregate potential of ego fulfilment of the society. With bigger funds, bigger governments can do more in that way. The temptation to call the tune if paying the piper is strong. But a purchased subjection to another's will is still subjection.

The foregoing observations clearly premise acceptance of individualism. So doing, they reject the pretentions of the *état-providence* and generally of policy planning to be good in themselves. Removal of situational roadblocks to personal expansion and traffic control to minimize collisions that such expansion involves are both legitimate state functions.

They are the legitimate state functions. Prescription of goals is not. However benevolently conceived, in imposing one set of values it suppresses others. Even if aimed at the general welfare, in its noble arrogance it is and must be a dictation of the preferences of a particular person or group. A case might be made for enforced conformity were their author an infallible judge of what is good. No one demonstrably is. The justification of liberty is not that it produces an ideal social arrangement but that, with no known test of what is ideal, it gives elbow room for a variety of views.

The dilemma of organizations, including governments, is that increased size, which increases power, thus enabling them to create new potentials of self-fulfilment, obscures particularisms. Thus it forecloses the exercise of those potentials. In great part, political history is the record of ongoing experiments to construct and maintain units with territorial and demographic dimensions reaching an appropriate compromise between the two. Small and feeble, they twinkle out or linger on as ineffective dwarfs. Large and strong, they become instruments for furthering the interests of some dominant element in the population; to it others are sacrificed. A wide spectrum of forms of political association, from leagues and alliances through personal or customs unions to federal states has evolved in response to these opposed perils. Success has been transitory at best. The fate of the looser types of association has tended to be dissolution, that of the stronger to be hegemony of the central establishment.[1] Sometimes starved, sometimes crushed, the achievement of personal goals is thwarted.

Thence grows Canada's current crisis. Beyond its immediate importance to Canadians, the response to its challenge involves the general problems of whether large-scale political entities can be made both workable and tolerable and if so how. Unless all concerned are disposed to

---

1   For an instructive discussion, see May, Decision making and stability in political systems, (1970), 3 *Can. J. Pol. Sci.* 73.

approach it in those terms, rather than preoccupied with an ad hoc reaction to current irritations, no durable accommodation is possible. In crafting an appropriate constitution, Canada can serve as a laboratory experiment in providing for political association continental in its dimensions of people culturally and economically diverse, which will enhance the exercise of choice for some and curtail it for none of the communities it embraces. The competence power-centres receive should permit but not exceed their respective qualifications for apt and effective dealing with circumstances so as to promote those ends.

Preoccupation with words has become an unfortunate obsession. On the one hand Canadian unity, on the other independence, are shibboleths. The former, with its connotation of uniformity even more clearly apparent in the variant 'Canadian identity' which signifies sameness, repudiates the variety that inescapably and invaluably has characterized the country. The latter, which bespeaks disjunction, is not present in pure form as between any two countries in our entangled world; still less is it possible in a social and geographic setting like Canada's, nor indeed is it sought even by those who preach it but who all also preach association of some, albeit a modified, sort. Each is, however, becoming a rallying cry. Certainly some loss of face will be involved on each side in abandoning sterile commitment to a slogan in favour of a common search for the elements of a viable association. But that is for a little while still not quite a forlorn hope.

In 1841 and again in 1867, schemes were elaborated and enacted with a view to settling the terms of association. They were limping and only temporary successes. As the Union of the Canadas required replacement with a radically different scheme, the present Confederation facing imminent collapse can, as an alternative to discard, be recast using the same materials. The shaping of a proper mould is indeed critically important. Mere repairs cannot make serviceable an instrument whose revealed deficiencies are in the basic pattern. Simple fragmentation, however, can produce nothing but a heap of non-working parts.

The primary objective of this book is to induce a fresh look. It proposes a new model, certainly not the only and maybe not even the best one conceivable but the best that I have been able to conceive. A modified or a quite different one may be preferable. I not only welcome but invite a competition of ideas which will result in the best product. That surely will not be a patched-up status quo. While much that appears may be reminiscent of provisions in the BNA Act 1867,[2] it should have to rest on its own merits having regard to the transformed association. Present provisions

2 30–31 Vict., c 3 (UK)

can give suggestions but they ought to be appraised in a wholly neutral spirit without a predisposition either to adopt or to avoid.

Necessarily detailed and complex, my sketch of a proposed new constitution still does not touch all the bases. About such major items as the Commonwealth and crown connection and commitment to the parliamentary form of government, nothing will be said; while any new constitution must deal with them, they do not bear on the locus of control within the Canadian community; determination of that can have the same consequences regardless of what is done about them. Silence regarding the amending process and its once-for-all analogue, the mechanics to use in framing and installing a new constitution, both critically important, finds its only excuse in an utter inability to come up with a recommendation. No existing federal constitution seems to furnish an inviting model nor is any of the variants so far proposed in Canada fully satisfactory. To achieve and to assure respect for an acceptable settled allocation of authority and yet meet the inevitable need for updating raises problems as regards both the organs for voicing assent and the required range of concurrence. My own feeling is that a preliminary exposure of projects to test popular reaction should be afforded somehow rather than leaving all depend on the unguided governments of the day, and that the level of approval somewhere between majority and unanimity should be fixed high enough to legitimate the result as a genuine common mandate. I suggest we should start from these postulates but their development has me baffled. Neither the details of executive and legislative structure nor transitional provisions generally are dealt with. They will be needed in order to get any new system going but by and large have slight impact on the nature of the ensuing association of Canadian societies. A possible exception is whether to continue the Senate. The function of a second chamber in a parliamentary system is ambiguous so that the decision would seem to depend largely on whether such a system should be retained, a matter bypassed for the reason noted.

A plan with those not inconsiderable omissions cannot pretend to completeness. It can nevertheless cover those matters which shape the substance of partnership. On all of these something will be said. The most obvious is the distribution of authority between the central and the member governments. It has virtually monopolized discussion and, in so doing, has left other critical areas unexplored. Attention will be given to restructuring the judicial system[b] and to a proposal for managing access to revenues. Suggestions will be made for additions to the very meagre existing specification of the relations between the members. What kind of

---

b A chapter on the judicial system did not form part of the manuscript.

constitutional status if any should be given to civil liberties, as also to municipalities, has attracted and will receive some comment.[c] So the coverage though partial is not narrow.

The focus is specifically Canadian. The perspective is not.

Assuming the general propositions advanced at the outset to be valid, the recommendations here and the supporting argument are relevant to any political association on a large scale or of diverse communities, at least in the western world. Widespread signs of malaise are symptoms of a bad fit between today's mass societies and the governments they have inherited. Ordinary people are coming to suffer and often to resent government as somebody out there shoving them about in a way heedless of their aspirations and felt needs. Nearly everyone accepts that a society cannot exist without some means of exercising collective authority, hence some person or group of persons as power bearers. But unless others see them as not acting just on them but for them, only submission will ensue, perhaps resigned, perhaps rankling. So too, unless the power exercised and those collective interests whose furtherance legitimates its possession are rationally connected. The proposals to be made aim to relate Canadian power bearers more directly to the persons over whom or the collective functions for which they have authority and thereby, it is hoped, to have the institutions of government be and be seen as the instruments of shared social purposes. As projections of principle, though doubtless not for detailed imitation, they can serve beyond our borders as suggestions for coping with the problem of citizen alienation in democratic states.

It works both ways. We can find guidance from others as well as suggesting ideas to them. Where the method of controlled experiments is not feasible, the multiform patterns of political combination are a partial substitute. Different results have been derived from similar terms; similar results have been reached under and even rested on different terms; aspects of intergovernmental relations neglected in some constitutions have been spoken to in others.

A comparison of verbal text with applied consequences in several settings can teach something about framing apt provisions. The United States and Australia are the obvious referents. The common and the distinctive features of other instruments of state association may on occasion usefully supplement them. The extent of concurrence on the assignment of competence between government levels reflects independent intuitions as to its appropriate location. A drift of effective power in the

---

c Chapters on civil liberties and the constitutional position of municipalities did not form part of the manuscript.

same direction away from the intended compromise division suggests a need for new structures to counter deficiencies or biases common to those provided.

A written fundamental charter is presupposed. Without that, no question of correspondence between statement and experience arises. It must moreover be a public-law analogue to articles of partnership. The written constitutions of unitary states have nothing to contribute to the design of a federation, however instructive they may be on such other things as the organs of representative democracy or civil liberties. Those are the only limits on the relevant field of inquiry although historical and cultural factors make some comparative materials more pertinent than others. We can borrow ideas hoping to repay.

To give lasting satisfaction, however, constitutions must be cut to the measure and styled to the taste of the wearers. That differs from society to society, reflecting the material and cultural milieu. On the world scene, a realization seems to be growing that what suits some may not suit others. Domestically, little attention has been given to distinctive conditioning circumstances. The structuring of an acceptable and viable constitution depends rather on what Canada is like than on what one personally would like.

The permanent distinctive features of Canada have been her geography and her diverse societies. Ours is a vast land with a marginal location and a small population.

To receive any consideration in the family of nations and, more important, to enjoy more than a mere subsistence economy, a political entity needs a minimum critical mass. This both presumes and allows a common authority with the capacity to marshall human and material resources so that all contribute to and all share in the pool. The concentration of private power consequent on our modern market economy can be matched and mastered only by political centres of comparable magnitude. Societies being, like physical bodies, subject to the laws of gravity, resistance to the pull exerted by a huge nearby mass depends on the exertion of a counterforce; the relevance of this for Canada is evident. Whether the united strength of Canada's people can suffice to meet the challenges of the other power structures, foreign or domestic, actual or potential, which circumstance our life has been doubted by some. In any event only such united strength would seem adequate. The minimum appropriate dimensions of federal power are dictated by that consideration.

The imperatives of physical geography and economic organization tell in one direction, those of history and mores in another. The two solitudes label oversimplifies the reality it dramatizes. Besides Quebec's, there are some four to at least ten, depending on how one looks at it, regions in

Canada with their own cultures, their own patterns of life and values, even of speech. The assumption in much that has been said and done is that Canada is just Ontario writ large. That is wrong. Even a brief acquaintance with Victoria and Corner Brook – and many places in between – would prove that. The world over, even national and in a still greater degree regional traits have been blurred. Canadians have not escaped. Yet they are by no means homogenized. Although even within provinces accepted ways of behaving and thinking differ among sections, the differences are smaller than in the country as a whole. The more a central authority undertakes to impose a common standard on the relations and conduct of individuals in the ordinary affairs of daily life, the more a sense of alienation from the institutions of government grows. To avoid endemic discontent, power over such matters must be dispersed among power centres having at least a rough correspondence with the diverse social milieus. That diversity of regional social attitudes is a blessing to be promoted and preserved.

The disparity in material resources is on the other hand a curse. The 1867 Act tried to do something about it but with only ephemeral success because the static solutions proposed became obsolete over time. It has never ceased to inspire agitation and legislation. To urge a uniform income level throughout Canada would be chimerical. If one were realized it would more likely be a swamp than a plateau. But there can be no happy partnership between plutocrat and pauper. Depressed areas are a drain on the national vigour. Their elimination is a legitimate, even an imperative national concern.

These three sets of conditions – the need for consolidating a certain amount of power in order to command respect from the economic and the international systems, complicated as it is by our large area and relatively small population; the distinctive sense of identity of the various regions; the uneven distribution of wealth – are the background factors to reckon with in structuring a workable division of functions between the provincial and the federal levels.[3] Indeed that would appear to have been the basic premise of the 1867 Act. But it was an inarticulate premise. A random listing of minutiae misled later generations into approaching that act not as a system but as a mere heap of items. Like it, what I would propose grounds itself on those three factors; it tries to bring into clearer relief their importance as the shaping principles of our national consensus.

3 Johnson, The dynamics of federalism in Canada, (1968), 1 *Can. J. Pol. Sci.* 18, is a valuable discussion of these elements, particularly the differentiating factors among Canadian societies; however, it neglects somewhat the peculiarities of physical and political geography which provide the parameters for federal authority.

A federal system is one in which there coexist a central or common and member governments, both of them possessing authority not derived from nor immediately exercised through the other.

One can hardly envisage two governments with a universal concurrent plenitude of authority over a population. Redundancy certainly and discordance probably would characterize such a regime. Its historical absence shows the impracticability of that arrangement. Every instance known to me of bipolar jurisdictional legitimacy has been marked by an attempt at specification of the sphere of competence of one or both of the recognized power centres.

The limitations of language prevent any specification from being either complete or precise. No catalogue of instances ever exhausts its set of possibilities; even were it possible to think of all currently existing matters, as it seldom if ever is, the relative rigidity needed to give any crystallized category distinctive content is incompatible with the infinite potential variations in fact complexes over time. Some overlooked or latent margin inevitably remains. On the other hand no verbal expression is a laser beam. A diffuse penumbra surrounds the core of meaning. The permissible range for the exercise of any specified power may thus run into situations where the other level of government also has acted by virtue of a basis of authority belonging to it. Some rule must be provided for deciding which shall prevail. The specification of spheres of competence has to be supplemented either expressly or by construction with principles assigning the unitemized residuum and prescribing priority where both levels have validly acted.

The questions of residual power and of paramountcy or supersedure are important features of the context within which the particular powers belonging to each level operate. Discussion of them preliminary to the proposal of particular powers is appropriate.[d]

It has been customary to talk of levels of government and I shall throughout use that familiar term just because it is familiar. Unfortunately it lends itself to the connotation that one is of superior dignity to the other. That implication should not be attached to anything that will be said. In Canada the members are styled 'provinces.' That too has been felt to be demeaning. But nothing of substance would seem to turn on the name, whether 'province,' 'state,' 'canton,' or 'land.' Each is a mere tag for a member unit of a federation. For home use, any member can use whatever it finds more comfortable. Uniformity is unnecessary, as witness

---

d While the chapter on the residuary power follows, a chapter dealing with paramountcy did not form part of the manuscript. The proposal with respect to paramountcy is set out supra, at 6.

the fact that some of the United States prefer to call themselves 'commonwealths' rather than states. However, employment of some single term in treatment of them as a class avoids textual clumsiness. To that end only, the partners in Canada will be spoken of using the accustomed expression, 'provinces.' In each case, conventional practice is observed wholly as a matter of literary convenience with no overtones as to status intended.

2 THE PROVINCIAL RESIDUARY POWER[a]

PROPOSED PROVISION
Each provincial legislature may make laws operative within the province as to anything not assigned by section (   ) to parliament. This power extends but is not limited to laws dealing with

1 The constitution of the province.
2 Municipal and local authorities.
3 The raising of money by any mode or system of taxation.
4 Civil and criminal law and procedure without prejudice to the power of parliament to provide for carrying out measures enacted in the exercise of powers given it by this Constitution.

The existence of non-hierarchical political units partitioning the universe of authority over a single population, which is the fundamental feature of federalism, calls for clarification of their respective spheres of competence. Hence all federal constitutions undertake some spelling out, either for one or for both of the levels of government, of what falls to it or to them to deal with.

One pattern particularizes for a single level only; another does so for both.

The first is exemplified by the United States and the Australian constitutions. Article 1 of the former elaborates in section 8 what 'The Congress shall have power' to do with no comparable provision relating to the states. Likewise sections 51 and 52 of the Australian constitution give 'power to make laws for the peace, order and good government of the Commonwealth with respect to' thirty-nine and three heads respectively and leave the states' power amorphous. The main formal difference between these constitutions is that the Australian expresses that parliament's control over section 52 items is exclusive (with clause (iii) incorporating by reference 'other matters declared by this Constitution to be within the exclusive power of Parliament'), but does not for those in section 51, while the text of the United States constitution is silent on the matter. Significant determinancy is built into both systems by a concluding clause. In the United States, article 1, section 8, empowers congress 'to

---

a This chapter was not titled in the manuscript.

make all Laws which shall be necessary and proper for carrying into Execution the foregoing Powers and all other Powers vested by this Constitution in the Government of the United States or in any department or officer thereof.' In Australia, section 51 (xxxix) authorizes parliament to legislate with respect to 'matters incidental to the execution of any power vested by this constitution in the Parliament, or in the Federal judicature, or in any department or officer of the Commonwealth.'

The BNA Act 1867 took the other track, specifying in sections 91 and 92 'classes of subjects' for parliament and the provincial legislatures, respectively, not indeed as roots of power but as measures for the legitimation of legislation which, as to 'matters coming within' the enumerations, was on the one hand for parliament, on the other for the provinces. There are thus two lists, each indistinctive, and they are mutually exclusive. Thus section 91 speaks of 'the exclusive Legislative Authority of the Parliament of Canada' 'in relation to all matters not coming within the classes of Subjects by this Act assigned exclusively to the Legislatures of the Provinces' and section 92 says 'In each Province the Legislature may exclusively make Laws,' etc. Sections 94A (old age and similar pensions) and 95 (agriculture and immigration) modify the general scheme by incorporating what amounts to a sparsely populated 'concurrent list.'

The single-list pattern always is a single federal list.[1] No known federal constitution has undertaken to list only provincial powers, leaving those of the federal government inchoate. The concept of residuary power characteristically supplies the basis for state and provincial authority – in the original United States constitution *sub silentio* but almost immediately by the adoption of the now disembowelled Tenth Amendment,[2] in Australia by virtue of section 107. The Swiss situation is of the same general type as is found in the United States and Australia but with differences in detail.[3]

A federal listing balanced by a residual power to members, while quite common, is often illusory.

Thus article 124 of the constitution of Mexico provides that 'The powers not expressly granted by this Constitution to federal officials are understood to be reserved to the States.' But article 73 gives to congress a list of exclusive powers which leaves the states little of any real moment and even that little is subject to a long list of exceptions attached to the

1 But cf the Republic of South Africa Constitution Act 1961, s 59(1), which does not set out a list of federal powers but merely states that 'Parliament ... shall have full power to make laws for the peace, order and good government of the Republic.'
2 The Tenth Amendment, ratified in 1791, is as follows: 'The powers not delegated to the United States by the Constitution, nor prohibited by it to the States, are reserved to the States respectively, or to the people.'
3 See Aubert, *Traité de droit constitutionnel suisse* I (1967), at 232–3, 241–2.

exercise of legislation. In the Federal German Republic, there is a bifurcated federal list, article 73 specifying exclusive and article 74 concurrent Bund legislative powers; article 70 provides that 'The Länder shall have the power to legislate insofar as the Basic Law does not confer legislative power on the Federation' but the disqualification is modified by the distinction that, for article 73 subjects, the länder can legislate 'only if and to the extent that a Federal law explicitly so authorizes them,' while they may as to article 74 subjects 'as long as and to the extent that the Federation does not use its legislative powers.' The comprehensiveness, approaching exhaustiveness, of the lists in articles 73 and 74 and the circumstance that the conditions for valid länder legislation embodied in these articles are seldom met has meant, however, that there is only a narrow range open to them. Much the same situation exists in Austria. The constitution of the USSR is the prime example of a nominal member-residual power swallowed up by an almost all-encompassing federal list.

The pattern of plural lists presents many variations in detail.

The model of two exclusive lists with the residue left to be distributed as local or common concerns predominate seems unique to Canada, probably because only here is the initial inquiry as to the matter of the legislation rather than the ambit of competence.

A different approach of some recent federal constitutions has been the elaboration of three lists – a federal list, a state list, and a concurrent list. Each level is authorized to legislate within its own designated list and both are competent as to matters on the concurrent list – always with the paramountcy principle applicable. This is the technique, for example, in the constitutions of India, article 246(1), and of Malaysia, article 74(1). They differ, however, in that in India, under article 248(1), 'Parliament has exclusive power to make law with respect to any matter not enumerated in the state list or the concurrent list' while in Malaysia, article 77, 'The Legislature of a State has power to make laws with respect to any matter not being a matter with respect to which Parliament has authority to make laws.'

Single or plural, the lists, being words, are perforce only nuclear indications of the situations entrusted to the designated level. For any given case their coverage must be determined. For things found to fall outside the scope of all of them, some principle must be established as to which level is in charge. While it will not wholly eliminate, a broad reading of the specifics will shrink, that array, at the extreme to insignificance. The unspecified concerns being a reciprocal of those specified, provisions for settling the ambit of the latter interact with those assigning the former. Their natural association creates a risk of their being muted. Failure to observe the distinction so as to keep in view that there are two separate though related notions involved has generally stunted the residual area by reason of the favour shown on expanded reading of the specific grants. Particularly where, as in the United States and Australia, there is explicit textual recognition of the propriety of flexibility in application of the powers granted the federal government, no reliance can be placed on a forthright reservation of everything else to the members.

The US record is especially useful because there the issues were most consciously and elaborately confronted. For want of earlier models, the colonies at the time of the Revolution undertook to invent a plan of association and to spell out systematically how much of their newly claimed sovereignty each of them was prepared to put in the common pot. There had indeed been a variety of leagues and confederacies, which were in a sense rudimentary federations; but these had been established by undertaking individual commitments to each other, rather like treaties, and lacked both an integrated constitutional instrument and an authoritative expounder for one had it existed. The new sovereigns, with a revolutionary war to wage in common, understood the need for a common authority as to it. Moreover they recognized the utility of an integrated policy on such non-military matters as foreign affairs, currency, and the post office. These they were agreed could be centrally regulated. But they were not ready to relinquish any jurisdiction beyond that stated as being given. In first draft, the articles of confederation contented themselves with itemizing powers congress should have. Nothing was said as to incidental power, nor was there any reference to state authority. On the premise that a fence is a better protection against trespass than a mere statement of calls in a deed, an amendment was accepted that 'Each state retains its sovereignty, freedom and independence, and every Power, Jurisdiction and right, which is not by this confederation expressly delegated to the United States, in Congress assembled.'[4] An arrangement which incorporated a prototype of the Tenth Amendment but none of the 'necessary and proper' clause thus was an element in the mental climate when the Philadelphia convention assembled in 1787.

Features other than the allocation of power between congress and the states chiefly determined that convention's choice of the large-state Randolph plan over the Paterson small-state one. The two did differ in their treatment of the matters under consideration, but rather in style of expression than in substance.

The Paterson plan's generously descriptive language empowering congress 'to make laws ... in all cases which may concern the common interests

4 Articles of Confederation and Perpetual Union, art II

of the Union' seems at least as comprehensive as the 'necessary and proper' formula. But it was subject to the qualification that the power was 'not to interfere with the government of the individual states, in any matters of internal police, which respect the government of such states only, and wherein the general welfare of the United States is not concerned.'[5] It thus adverted even if elliptically to both notions – congressional flexibility and reservation to the states.

The Randolph plan left the latter to whatever inference might be drawn from its specification of national legislative authority as extending to 'the Legislative Rights vested in Congress by the Confederation; and moreover to ... all Cases for the general Interest of the Union, and ... to which the States are separately incompetent, or in which the Harmony of the United States may be interrupted by the Exercise of individual Legislation.'[6] It took as a start the situation existing under the articles of confederation but expanded to include other matters defying effective state control or fraught with interstate friction and broadly 'for the general interests of the Union.' The last seems prima facie as open-ended as the Paterson formula. Any occasion for its two companions is hard to see, unless they imply some feeling that 'the general interests of the Union' did not embrace them, and should be read in some not too apparent restricted sense. In any case, the primary referent was the familiar established division under the articles, itself shaped by the reservation clause. Its use in that capacity might be thought to carry a built-in limitation modifiable only by affirmatively establishing one of the annexed conditions. On that assumption the Randolph plan need not and did not allude to state reservation.

The choice between the plans left a conforming text to be elaborated. The approval plan was referred to a committee on detail. That committee's report spelled out as congressional powers substantially those now appearing in article I, section 8, amplifying considerably the articles of confederation list. It may be surmised that many of them were seen as detailing items where either state ineffectiveness or interstate conflict was apprehended. For others, the 'general interest of the Union' may have been the sole justification. In the aggregate, their source in a committee of detail indicates that they were designed as a particularization of the general directives in the Randolph plan as to the content of congressional power. They concluded with the necessary and proper clause in its present form. There being no published committee reports, one cannot know how the phrasing was arrived at or what relation its author (authors?) saw

5 Fanaud, *Records of the Federal Convention of 1787*, II, at 21.
6 Ibid, at 131–2

it as having to the listed powers. It was agreed to too late in the wearied convention's proceedings, apparently after scant separate deliberation, and is unnoticed in any account of the convention debates.

Lively discussions both in pamphlets and in the state ratifying conventions compensate for the convention's delphic dealing. Some bore on the necessary and proper clause, some on the silence about state powers, some on both. The argument mainly relied on to allay the fears occasioned by the former and to excuse the departure of the latter from the articles of confederation was that the powers of congress were limited to those delegated. Private law analogies to an agent's express authority, to the granting clauses in deeds, and to specific bequests in wills were adduced as relevant. Again and again it was emphasized that every state power not comprised within the delegations was left untouched with no accretion of power to congress beyond those delegations.

Not questioning that, critics still were uneasy lest the terms as they stood encourage the natural tendency to expand a granted authority to its outside limits. Dependence on delegation as a limitation could be read two ways – either that everything was retained that was not given away or that only that was retained which was not given away. The important question of which was the subtrahend and which the remainder went unexamined. Tests or examples were set out to indicate the range of undelegated powers. Those favouring the draft intimated vaguely that the states would continue to control the whole heap of things represented in their current legislation while congress would be restricted to a few set aside for it with fairly clear contours.

In the end the instrument was ratified as it stood. Many states assented only grudgingly, often stating that they did so on the understanding that existing state powers remained and serving notice of an intention to bring forward amendments to insert a clause like the second article of confederation. Ordinarily they tracked its language of retaining everything not 'expressly' or 'clearly' delegated. Virginia alone omitted such an adverb. That probably reflected the influence of Madison whose observations in *The Federalist* are the only discovered instance where exception was taken to its use. Others supporting the theory that delegation was intrinsically a reservation read it as already operating just like the provision in the articles. But it was left to Madison to bring forward the proposal for amendments satisfying the desires of the states in the course of ratification. And so the one that became the Tenth Amendment left out 'expressly' and said only 'delegated.'

That far were the residuary powers left floating in the original constitution anchored. But even while the amendments were awaiting a congressional vote, it was evident that the anchor might not hold. Hamilton's bill for incorporating the Bank of the United States was concurrently pending. Its constitutionality was questioned by, among others, Madison who deplored 'the diffusive and ductile' interpretation[7] of the necessary and proper clause and invoked his incipient Tenth Amendment and the state resolutions specifying an express delegation as being of the same tenor and indicating congressional intrusion in a reserved field. The Bank bill's supporters, no longer under the prudent restraint which had been maintained to get the constitution adopted, acknowledged that 'that was so if the letter of the Constitution was to be adhered to.'[b] They did not accept that it was, nor even, the utmost position taken in the debates attending ratification, that one needed to point to some delegated power whose full realization was sensibly connected with the legislation proposed. Their position was that 'by the very nature of government, the legislature had an implied power of using every means, not positively prohibited by the Constitution, to execute the ends for which that government is instituted'[b] and that those ends were expressed in the preamble as being the 'common defence and general welfare,' the carrying into execution of which was the measure of the powers with which congress was invested. Foreshadowing the Privy Council's reasoning in *John Deere Plow Co* v *Wharton*,[8] the argument was advanced that, since no state could establish a national bank, the power rested in the national legislature. Congress proceeded to approve both the Bank bill and the Tenth Amendment.

Although strictly speaking all this went only to the effect of the necessary and proper clause, uncomplicated by the existence of a Tenth Amendment still in process of gestation, the immateriality of the latter was early manifested. Marshall cj, writing for the Supreme Court in *McCulloch* v *Maryland*,[9] emphasized the omission of 'expressly' from the amendment, which he read as having virtually no independent operative effect; instead, he stressed the 'necessary and proper' clause, characterized by him as 'an additional power not a restriction on those already granted,'[10] a position plainly contrary to what had been originally said. The 'motive for its insertion' being 'the desire to remove all doubts respecting the right to legislate on that vast mass of incidental powers which must be involved in the constitution, if that instrument be not a splendid bauble,'[11] 'necessary and proper' did not import necessity but

---

7 Clarke & Hall, *Legislative and Documentary History of the Bank of the United States* (1832), at
   42
b The sources of these quotations could not be located.
8 [1915] A.C. 330
9 (1819) 4 Wheat. 316
10 Ibid, at 420
11 Ibid, at 420–1

rather, in a much-quoted passage: 'Let the end be legitimate, let it be within the scope of the constitution, and all means which are appropriate, which are plainly adopted to that end, which are not prohibited, but consist with the letter and spirit of the constitution are constitutional.'[12]

That approach has, with some oscillation, prevailed. The amendment is now almost a dead letter, the 'necessary and proper' clause a shift of the residual power to congress. The position has been summarized as follows:

> The amendment *states but a truism* that all is retained which has not been surrendered. There is nothing in the history of its adoption to suggest that it was more than declaratory of the relationship between the national and state governments *as it had been established before the amendment* or that its purpose was other than to allay fears that the new national government might seek to exercise powers not granted, or that the states might not be able to exercise fully their reserved powers. From the beginning and for many years the amendment has been construed as not depriving the national government of authority to resort to all means for the exercise of a granted power which are appropriate and plainly adopted to the permitted end.[13]

The vestigial character of the 'reserved powers' alluded to is shown by the observation that the amendment, though characterized as a truism, 'is not without significance. The Amendment expressly declares the constitutional policy that Congress may not exercise power in a fashion that impairs the States' integrity or their ability to function effectively in a federal system.'[14] One must respect their claim to continued existence but not to do anything in particular.[15]

Even had meaningful content been given to the amendment and an interpretation more in line with the ordinary rules of agency law to the 'necessary and proper' clause, the evolution of some of the delegations, notably the commerce power and the spending power, would suffice and has in fact been used to sustain congressional absorption of many areas of authority and corresponding displacement of the states. The expansive potential of such clauses is a separate question which need only be noted here and will be discussed later.[c] The Fourteenth Amendment's due process and equal protection clauses too, have foreclosed much state

---

12 Ibid, at 421
13 *U.S.* v *Darby* (1941) 312 U.S. 100, at 124 (emphasis added)
14 *Fry* v *U.S.* (1975) 421 U.S. 542, at 547
15 But cf *National League of Cities* v *Usery* (1976) 426 U.S. 833, holding that congress may not constitutionally prescribe minimum wages for state employees; in attempting to do so, congress had 'sought to wield its power in a fashion that would impair the States' "ability to function effectively in a federal system"' (at 852, per Rehnquist J).
c The commerce and spending clauses were to be examined in the uncompleted chapter 7, The Inflation and Deflation of Federal Competence.

policy choice although little use has been made of their authorization of congressional action; since, being posterior to the Tenth, it amended that as well as other portions of the constitution, a clearer case can be made here than for swollen readings of the pre-existing delegations. With no similar terms in the BNA Act, a consideration of their consequences is more pertinent to the subsequent examination of what might be the place for such provisions in a future Canadian constitution.[d] Whatever the impact of provisions additional to an expressed limitation of the central legislature to delegated powers, the US experience demonstrates that the latter is illusory as a means of maintaining residuary power in the member legislatures.

Australia's is consistent. Sections 51(xxxix) and 107 are rough equivalents of the 'necessary and proper' clause and the Tenth Amendment respectively.[16] Despite shades of difference, the language and its operation is very similar in the two countries.

Neither section attracted serious discussion at the conferences which finally drew up the proposed constitution for submission to the imperial parliament. The basic decision to incorporate something of the sort had been made long before. Its implementation in appropriate language was a matter of drafting detail. The critical choice, made at a precursor conference in 1891, was in favour of following the US and rejecting the Canadian model of allocating power between the central government and the members. Throughout the long gestation of the constitution, the continuation of state functioning as it stood save for specific transfers to the federal government was an accepted feature. To the US delegations, additions were made, some lifted from section 91 of the BNA Act,[17] but others which, by mentioning things that the United States Supreme Court later read as comprised within congressional power under article 1, section 8, the Australians seemed to feel would otherwise not be open to federal control.

d A chapter dealing with entrenching protection for civil liberties did not form part of the manuscript.

16 The sections read as follows:

51 The Parliament shall, subject to this Constitution, have power to make laws for the peace, order, and good government of the Commonwealth with respect to: –
(xxxix) Matters incidental to the execution of any power vested by this Constitution in the Parliament or in either House thereof, or in the Government of the Commonwealth, or in the Federal Judicature, or in any department or officer of the Commonwealth.

107 Every power of the Parliament of a Colony which has become or becomes a State, shall, unless it is by this Constitution exclusively vested in the Parliament of the Commonwealth or withdrawn from the Parliament of the State, continue as at the establishment of the Commonwealth, or at the admission or establishment of the State, as the case may be.

17 Eg, marriage and divorce (s 51 (xxi), (xxii)) and bills of exchange and promissory notes (s 51(xvi)).

Curtailment of state concerns was by way of a more generous list of federal powers, not by a more generous construction than that supposed to exist in the United States.

Although that US pattern was the basic model, the language was not identical and indeed slightly different formulations appeared as the constitution evolved.

The counterpart of the 'necessary and proper' clause was changed only a little. The Tenth Amendment's analogue had a more tortuous history.[18] There was general concern at the earlier stages with what the members would be losing as contrasted with the US approach through what the central government was to receive. This resulted in less compact formulas even with the Amendment's reservation of anything 'to the people' dropped.[19] In its eventual form, section 107[20] accommodates the recognized contingency of new states while keeping the perspective of a mass of state powers from which subtractions are made.

Neither section attracted the public discussion in depth which had attended their US precursors. This lack of contemporaneous materials was measurably compensated by subsequent observations in judicial opinions showing the thinking of participants in the constitutional deliberations.

In the United States where there remained on the Supreme Court, when it first dealt with the matter, no one except Marshall who had been actively involved in the making of the constitution, his original aberrant approach, echoed in *McCulloch v Maryland*[21] would have for his colleagues the weight due his having been on the scene.[22] In contrast, all the initial High Court appointees had been actors, two of them leading actors, in the development of the constitution. Prepared at the outset to refer directly to what was then done[23] they were quickly squelched by Privy Council insistence on the blinkered rule of not considering legislative history.[24] This precluded further frank invocation. It could not erase the events from the memory of the High Court justices nor does it deprive their remarks of significance as reflecting that memory. What complicates the record is that that court was divided. Griffith and Barton, who had played a role as draftsmen, joined with O'Connor to write majority judgments

18 See generally, La Nauze, *The Making of the Australian Constitution* (1972).
19 While I have found no discussion of this omission, it may have been thought inapposite in an instrument which was to emanate not from 'we the people' but from the imperial parliament.
20 Supra note 16
21 (1819), 4 Wheat. 316
22 All the more so since Madison's notes had not been published and the fugitive materials like pamphlets and ratifying discussions in the states would not have been readily accessible to or used by counsel or court, except for *The Federalist Papers*.
23 *D'Emden v Pedder* (1904) 1 C.L.R. L.R. 91. Cf *Deakin v Webb* (1904) 1 C.L.R. 585
24 *Webb v Cottrim* [1907] A.C. 81

from which Higgins and Isaacs, secondary and even peripheral members of the constitutional conventions, dissented. The latter two, however, outlived their brethren, Isaacs by many years, and with the lapse of time their analysis supplanted the Griffith-Barton views. It is the latter, however, that, coming from those who had so much to do with choosing the language, constitute the nearest equivalent to the US pamphlets and ratifications as the most authentic revelations of contemporary understanding.

The ongoing judicial dialogue reflected in general the ideas to be found in the US materials with an occasional new wrinkle added but the old ambiguity retained.

Section 107 was, as Griffith saw it, designed as a paraphrase of the Tenth Amendment and section 51(xxxix) of the 'necessary and proper' clause[25] – 'language not verbally identical but synonymous.'[26] Barton as to the latter thought the Australian provision 'at least as wide as,' 'probably an ampler one.'[27] The verbal changes were basically just that, with perhaps a slight indefinite shade of difference as to section 51(xxxix); the change in wording did not trace to any specific or substantial changes in meaning. That was not questioned by any one. Nor was it elucidated, doubtless because each could understand it in the uncertain light the extant materials allowed him to attribute to the US terms.

Almost nothing more was then said about section 107 – certainly nothing giving it any operative effect. Griffith CJ did indeed comment that no exceptions could be made from a reservation of power to the states; but the reservation at issue derived from a negative pregnant in a specific grant, not from 107's broad language.[28] In the sole extended discussion, Isaacs J said, 'Of itself it reserves nothing ... [and] has nothing to do with cutting down Commonwealth powers ... I consider section 107 of no effect in determining the extent of the Commonwealth power,'[29] an observation which Griffith and Barton suffered to pass unchallenged. So stating, he anticipated the US dismissal of the Tenth Amendment as 'stat[ing] but a truism.'[30]

It was section 51(xxxix) that received most attention as an attempt at containment of federal power.

Obviously the relationship between a federally specified head of power and a legislative provision on something which would not at first blush be seen as one of its elements is what both the 'necessary and proper' clause

25 *D'Emden* v *Pedder*, supra note 23, at 94, 105; *Deakin* v *Webb*, supra note 25, at 605
26 *Deakin* v *Webb*, supra note 23, at 606
27 *Huddart, Parker & Co Pty Ltd* v *Moorehead* (1909) 8 C.L.R. 330, at 364; *Jumbunna Coal Mine* v *Victoria Coal Miners' Association* (1907) 6 C.L.R. 309, at 344
28 *A.-G. N.S.W.* v *Brewery Employees Union of N.S.W.* (1908) 6 C.L.R. 469, at 503
29 *Australian Steamships Ltd* v *Malcolm* (1914) 19 C.L.R. 298, at 330
30 *U.S.* v *Darby*, supra note 13

and the 'incidental' power under section 51(xxxix) are all about. The place of each and the intimacy of their connection are both of them factors. To the latter the Australians alone manifested sensitivity.

The main concern, the centre of gravity of legislation, it was suggested, must be within the terms of the grant, and extensions beyond them must be subsidiary to that central theme. 'The exercise of the incidental and supplemental power must be for the execution of some law passed under the principal power and not, so to speak, in the air.'[31] There was a tendency to describe the appropriate position in language familiar to Canadian law[32] as 'ancillary'[33] – a formulation which would be more enlightening were the meaning of that term better settled.[34] What it obscurely points to is the need for distinguishing the primary matter of the legislation, its pith and substance, from its secondary features. Only if federal as to pith and substance will other matters dealt with be sustainable as incidental. So spoke the judges who had been involved in the drafting process; the other wing of the court did not see or at least did not discuss the problem of dominance and subordination[35] following in this the us precedents.

What should be the challenged legislation's functional utility for the effectuation of a delegated power? Attempts to express what would suffice pointed in somewhat different directions, ranging from 'whatever is in the opinion of the legislature the most convenient'[36] even though it be neither 'helpful' nor 'conducive' to its execution but 'merely consequential' on it[37] to a requirement that the connection be 'direct, substantial and proximate.'[38] It is not quite clear how far these are consistent with each other or how they corresponded with propositions on which there was general agreement. No more than in the United States need the particular measure be indispensably requisite to the execution of the delegation[39] as was clearly indicated by replacement of the word 'necessary' by 'inciden-

31 *Australian Steamships Ltd v Malcolm*, supra note 29, at 308 (per Griffiths CJ dissenting)
32 The expression, first applied to the BNA in *A.-G. Ont. v A.-G. Can.* [1894] A.C. 189, has been a commonplace of judicial discourse.
33 See *Huddart, Parker & Co Pty Ltd v Moorehead*, supra note 27, at 334 (per Griffiths CJ), 366 (per Barton J); *Jumbunna Coal Mine v Victoria Coal Miners' Association*, supra note 27, at 345 (per Barton J), 356 (per O'Connor J); *Australian Steamships Ltd v Malcolm*, supra note 29, at 312 (per Barton J dissenting).
34 For the sloppy way it has been used, see *Laskin's Canadian Constitutional Law* (4th ed rev Abel 1975), at 19. See Abel, The neglected logic of 91 and 92, (1969), 19 *U.T.L.J.* 487, at 492, for an attempt to bring order into this chaos along the lines suggested in the text.
35 But cf *Huddart, Parker & Co Pty Ltd v Moorehead*, supra note 27, at 410–11 (per Higgins J)
36 *D'Emden v Pedder*, supra note 23, at 94 (per Griffiths CJ)
37 *R v Kidman* (1915) 20 C.L.R. 425 (per Gavan Duffy and Rich JJ)
38 *Australian Steamships Ltd v Malcolm*, supra note 29, at 321 (per Barton J dissenting).
39 *Jumbunna Coal Mine v Victoria Coal Miners' Association*, supra note 27, at 343–5 (per Barton J), 376 (per Isaacs J); *Australian Steamships Ltd v Malcolm*, supra note 29, at 312 (per Barton J dissenting).

tal.' Marshall's statement in *McCulloch* v *Maryland*[40] was adopted as the applicable principle.[41] But its grand rhetoric left room for difference as to what it meant. Some, as had been true of the 'necessary and proper' clause, saw section 51(xxxix) as no more than a redundant reassurance of what would have been implied anyway.[42] Isaacs J flatly disagreed. For him, every express grant gives 'by implication every ancillary power that is necessary to ... the proper exercise of the direct power it is intended to execute,' but he could 'not agree that it [section 51(xxxix)] adds nothing to the Parliamentary power which would not be implied if it were omitted"'; it was 'an independent power of legislation as high as any of the preceding thirty-eight in section 51.'[43] That analysis did not quite dispense with the need for companioning its use within some other power; but it did mean that it need not rest on that but had independent vitality. It thus conformed with the position of the proponents of the Bank bill that furtherance of the general ends of government could justify its use.[44]

In any event the delegated powers came into the picture alike for section 107 and section 51(xxxix). Whether 107 only disposed of the leftovers after those powers were fully fed or whether the states kept in their cupboards everything currently not listed on parliament's bill of fare, the scope must be determined. Whether 51(xxxix) recited or fortified or supplemented their intrinsic effect, it must be determined. Just as in the United States, differing opinions as to the constitutionality of particular federal laws have from the outset involved different constructions of the federal grants. They have been the general starting point, to be followed by an inquiry into how much rigidity or fluidity the clauses under consideration imported. Their imprecision lent itself to a diversity of views which was strikingly similar in both countries despite differences in phrasing.

Later development too has followed much the same course of virtual elimination of section 107 as an operative provision and disuse of section

40 Supra note 9
41 *Australian Steamships Ltd* v *Malcolm*, supra note 29, at 312 (per Barton J dissenting), 337 (per Powers J); *Federated Sawmill, etc Employees Association of Australia* v *James Moore & Sons Pty Ltd* (1909), 8 C.L.R. 466, at 510 (per O'Connor J); *Jumbunna Coal Mine* v *Victoria Coal Miners' Association*, supra note 27, at 321 (per Higgins J)
42 *R* v *Kidman*, supra note 37, at 433 (per Griffiths CJ); *Australian Steamships Ltd* v *Malcolm*, supra note 29, at 312 (per Barton J dissenting)
43 *R* v *Kidman*, supra note 37, at 440–1
44 That notion is also implied in Isaacs J's statement earlier in *Jumbunna Coal Mine* v *Victoria Coal Miners' Association*, supra note 27, at 376, that 'unless it can be shown that Parliament has infringed some positive restriction or prohibition of the Constitution, or has enacted as incidental to a main power some provision which no reasonable man could in any conceivable circumstances honestly regard as incidental, no Court has, in my opinion, any justification for attempting to review the action of the legislature and declaring that to be impossible of attainment, which Parliament has in its discretion thought and declared to be *desirable for the public welfare*.' (Emphasis added)

51(xxxix) as being in large part superfluous. The turning point came with the *Engineers' Case*.[45] The opinion for the court was by Isaacs J who together with Higgins J alone remained of the original bench.[46] There was no reference to section 51(xxxix), while section 107 was summarily disposed of by observing that it did not 'cut down' parliament's listed powers. Since then, as under the now prevailing practice in the United States, there has been an almost exclusive concentration on what the named grants to parliament (or congress), read in the largest sense, could extend to, considered by themselves without reference to incidentals or reservations.[47] One may wonder how comfortable those who had contended that having only delegated powers was in itself a confinement of federal authority would have been with delegations read so expansively. Clearly that approach left almost no occasion for section 51(xxxix) or the 'necessary and proper' clause and very little scope for section 107 or the Tenth Amendment.

The trace of life recognized as remaining in the Tenth Amendment to save it from debasement to a 'truism'[48] has its Australian equivalent in the limitation that parliament's powers cannot be exercised so as to abolish or destroy the states or such powers as they have.[49] The states may be eviscerated. They cannot be eliminated. The more perceptive analysis in Australia, however, rests this result on the general fabric of the commonwealth as being a federation rather than relying specifically on section 107. The minimal constraints on federal legislative power seem to be identical in extent. They do not go beyond the preservation of a formally federal structure. That much would surely be required independent of and without any expression of reservation of powers.

As for section 51(xxxix) and the necessary and proper clause, nothing currently flows from either.[50] Although US judgments still make occa-

---

45   *Amalgamated Society of Engineers* v *Adelaide Steamship Co* (1920) 28 C.L.R. 129
46   'Isaacs J and Higgins J ... in 1920 in the *Engineers' Case* when Griffith CJ, Barton J and O'Connor J had gone from the Bench ... were able to lead a new generation of judges in overthrowing [early doctrine]': Anderson, The states and relations with the commonwealth, in Else-Mitchell, ed, *Essays on the Australian Constitution* (2nd ed 1961), at 101.
47   'This [commerce] power, like all others vested in Congress, is complete in itself, may be exercised to its utmost extent, and acknowledges no limitations other than are prescribed by the Constitution': *Gibbons* v *Ogden* (1824) 22 U.S. 1, at 196 (per Marshall CJ). This proposition was expressly accepted by Isaacs J in the *Engineers' Case*, supra note 45, at 146.
48   *U.S.* v *Darby*, supra note 13
49   *Melbourne Corporation* v *The Commonwealth* (1947) 74 C.L.R. 31
50   For an ingenious but unconvincing attempt to distinguish between them and between express and implied incidental powers under the Australian Constitution, see Wynes, *Legislative, Executive and Judicial Powers in Australia* (5th ed 1976), at 363; and for a similarly scholastic distinction between express and implied incidental powers see Lane, *Australian Constitutional Law* (1964), at 747.

sional cosmetic reference to the latter, the coverage of the listed powers is the crux of the matter in both countries. Australia still calls for there being a specifiable grant as against US characterizations of the 'necessary and proper' clause as itself an additional power requiring no such anchorage.

A less assertive federal legislature and a somewhat more economical judicial construction of the particular grants seem to have left more open to the states in Australia than in the United States, where the Fourteenth Amendment has been made into an added constraint on diverse policy preferences. Hence the central government is a trifle more and the states a bit less cramped but on grounds that have nothing to do with the parallel provisions discussed above. They have fallen into disuse in both countries.

The consequence has been applauded as allowing the accommodation of the constitution to the changing needs of an evolving society. But the task undertaken here is the purely descriptive one of specifying the consequences of including both a federal-incidental powers and a state-reserved powers clause in a constitution. The confluent Australian and US experience teaches that there are none. The reference to incidental powers is otiose, that to reserved powers is hollow. One cannot look to them to assure the member governments pervasive intangible regulatory competence subject only to compact discrete qualifications.

Switzerland provides some basis for thinking that a text preserving the member's position but silent as to federal incidental powers may have more effect. There article 3 of the constitution reads: 'Les cantons sont souverains en tant que leur souveraineté n'est pas limitée par la Constitution fédérale, et, comme tels, ils exercent tous les droits qui ne sont pas délégués au pouvoir fédéral.' The very comprehensive package of express federal powers, particularly the control as to civil and criminal law given in line with Continental Code tradition, the absence of judicial review of federal statutes for constitutionality and the easy access to constitutional amendment to add federal powers combine to strip the question of much practical importance. La doctrine, however, sees the clause as more than empty language. It is recognized that the cantons are not truly sovereign and it is accepted that the federal government has some implied powers. These are confined, though, to things touching the confederation as a political organism,[51] the choice of means comparable to that under ordinary principles of agency law for effectuating granted powers, and new functional equivalents that may be developed. The granted power may not be used simply as a convenient handle to grasp the direction of activities not integral to it.[52] The relationship recalls that

51 Eg, the designation of a national holiday and a national anthem.
52 Aubert, supra note 3, at 236–42.

proposed as to Canada in the statement that 'power arises by implication because such implied power is requisite to enable the Dominion fully to perform the legislative functions devolved upon it in relation to the designated subject or subjects.'[53] Only the three countries whose positions have been examined have much to teach about the efficacy of formulas assigning residual and incidental powers. Where, as in the Soviet Union or Mexico, a pervasive party apparatus directs the functioning of formal government mechanisms at both levels or, as in Brazil, the written constitution is subject and is subjected to suspension whatever be the nominal allocation, those complicating circumstances made their experience irrelevant.

Recurring to the former three, two clear conclusions and one less clear are justified:

1   The generality of a grant of federal competence has nothing to do with its having been created by way of delegation. The categories will be read expansively as authorizations, not restrictively as limitations.
2   Express statement of member retention of all the rest of legislative authority accomplishes nothing where, instead of leaving the existence of such incidental powers as may be involved in application to be inferred in interpreting those named, it is specifically affirmed.
3   It may be, where there is no such textual affirmation, that language designating the members as entitled to the general reservoir of regulatory power will establish the grants as exceptions subject to the standard narrowing construction for provisions of that character.

Draftsmen seeking to save fields for provincial action must therefore not rely on entrusting only delegated powers to federal authority.

They must avoid saying anything about annexed incidental powers.

It is partly with that in mind that it is proposed that no trace remain of the peace, order, and good government clause in section 91. Because of its chequered history, uncertain sweep, and disturbing potential, it would in any event call for reconsideration. More immediately, as section 92(16)'s counterpart for dividing residuary power, it has no place in a constitution based on all such power belonging to the provinces. Its retention would easily be taken as equivalent to a 'necessary and proper' clause undermining the primary role of the provinces.

They should distinctly repose the residual power in the provinces.

It would seem best to do this in a somewhat different and rather more positive way than that used in the United States and Australia. Those constitutions speak of reserving or continuing in the states powers not delegated to or vested in the federal government. This suggested or at

---

53 *Reference re Waters and Water Powers* [1929] S.C.R. 200, at 213 (per Duff CJ)

least supported the approach giving initial and independent attention to the possible range of federal powers, leaving for the states only the margin after that was exhausted. To follow that formula would invite the contention that their precedents should be followed with the same resultant inanition of the reservation.

Recourse to a different pattern at least lessens the weight of those precedents. It does more. It signals deliberate rejection of their doctrine in favour of giving some substance to the floating provincial power.

The constitution of Malaysia points the way in its provision that 'The Legislature of a State has power to make laws with respect to any matter not being a matter with respect to which Parliament has authority to make laws.'[54] Though not used, the dormancy is occasioned by the very full parliamentary list, not by depreciation of the constitutional provision. Both federal and state powers are stated as grants, the former narrow and specific, the latter general. Since they are simultaneous creations, determination of their respective scope calls for, instead of separate preliminary emphasis on the outside limits of the federal grants, as under the other formula, assessing their relative place in the constitutional scheme.

The provision proposed does include a limitation on provincial competence not expressed in the Malaysian analogue, namely, to laws 'operative within the province.' It thus continues a pervasive feature of section 92 of the BNA Act. Special considerations that may apply as to a member of the family of nations do not affect the traditional common law refusal of extraterritoriality to the legislative competence of a member of a federation. Granted that the limitation may represent constitutional commitment to a position somewhat at odds with recent fashionable ideas about conflict of laws, leaving each province to settle the consequences of conduct within its borders seems better calculated to promote interprovincial harmony than would allowing them to be ruled from outside.

Subject to that geographical constraint, the language of the proposed provision, read in context, affords a clearer indication that provincial competence is the rule and federal the exception than that found in any existing constitution. The distinction between reservation and grant has already been mentioned. The formula not found in the Malaysian constitution that provincial legislative power 'extends but is not limited to' the brief list of nominate powers employs terms conventionally used to confer extensive authority in order to make it wholly clear that the preceding sentence is not to be cut down by niggardly interpretation. Correspondingly, an effort is made to tighten up the federal delegations through whose extension the residual provincial power can be bled to death. In the

54 Constitution of Malaysia, art 77

United States 'The Congress shall have power'[55] to deal with a variety of subjects. In Australia, parliament has power to make laws 'with respect to'[56] lists of matters. In Canada, it may make laws 'in relation to'[57] matters not provincially assigned. The proposed new constitution for Canada, as will be seen hereafter,[e] would only authorize parliament to 'make laws *as to*' the named subjects. The laws must not just bear on but be a direct application of some delegated power to be sustainable. These are doubtless literary niceties easy to overlook or discount. But they tend to close foreseeable loopholes.

Keeping the federal list sparse and specific is the real safeguard.

Absolute precision is out of the question. Words are never anything but generalities to symbolize conceptual sets, inclusion within which must be determined for each situation as it arises. Those appropriate for constitutions, instruments both comprehensive and enduring, must be wide, to encompass the multiple contingencies and accommodate the unforeseeable evolution of events the society they govern will surely encounter. Yet they can and should direct even though they cannot confine the choices available to those to whom it falls to apply them.

A scattergun listing has obscured the guidance provided alike in Canada, Australia, and the United States. In my opinion there was in all three a similar fundamental agreement as to the appropriate roles of the central and the member governments, but a random cataloguing of the items deprived them of directional value. The shortened and structured list which will be proposed aims to channel interpretation of the federal grants within the bounds noted as calling for a central authority.

Will the tauter statement of federal power and the general grant to the provinces taken together suffice to stay the usual erosion of the latter? That depends inescapably on the orientation of the members of the tribunal with the final say as to constitutionality. Here that can only be recognized. Further on, there will be detailed a novel arrangement for countering the standard bias of a federal judiciary in favour of federal authority.[f]

The foregoing discussion has dealt only with how provincial authority over most activity may be maintained. That it should be has been assumed. It is as indicated in the preceding chapter the basic assumption of the whole constitutional fabric here proposed. The reverse assumption leaves a wide latitude of means – express assignment of authority over unenum-

---

55 US Constitution, art 1, s 8
56 Commonwealth of Australia Constitution Act, s 51
57 BNA Act, s 91
 e See the proposed powers of parliament, supra, at 5.
 f This topic was not addressed in any of the chapters included in the manuscript.

erated subjects to the federal parliament as in the constitution of India; making state power only the remainder after a cancerous federal sub-trahend particularly if the latter is stated to include incidental powers as in Australia and the United States; probably a grant of power to make laws for peace, order, and good government of the country unless that be qualified as in the BNA Act.

If there is clear agreement on the first assumption, it must be clearly asserted. That is what the text proposed seeks to do. It adopts '*plures in unum*' as a better model for Canadian confederation than '*e pluribus unum.*'

Parliament may make laws as to ...
4 The raising of money by any mode or system of taxation.

Each provincial legislature may make laws operative within the province
... dealing with ...
5 The raising of money by any mode or system of taxation except duties
on imports.

Trade commerce and intercourse among the provinces shall be absolutely free.

No lands or property belonging to Canada or to any province shall be liable to taxation.

The naive view of taxes is to see them as the device governments use to get the money to pay their living expenses. They are to a considerable extent that; but they are both less and more than that.

Antiquity and immediacy concur to bring about that way of looking at them.

Their function as a source of supply for the upkeep of kings marks both our ancestral histories. In England, the very origin of parliaments was intimately linked with the association of votes or grants of supply with petitions for royal assent to laws redressing grievances. In France, the introduction of tax farmers as entrepreneurial intermediaries between the royal revenue consumers and the producing populace was a main contributing cause to the revolution. The particulars of the historic connection are forgotten. The centuries-long conditioning to connect taxes and the material needs of governments persists.

It is compounded for each taxpayer by his own interface with tax collection. We feel directly the transfer from our purses to that of the government. Our experience is that almost all that comes to us as income flows out in payment of personal or business expenses. The same simple

---

a From the manuscript, it appears that this and the next two chapters were to comprise a part to be entitled 'Getting and Spending.'

anthropomorphism that confuses private and public deficit financing likens government intake and outgo to our own. Inexact analogy and inherited thought patterns thus combine to divert attention from discrepancies between taxes and disbursements for government operations.

For one thing, governments get money from other sources.

One – borrowing – is perhaps only an apparent exception. Save for the catastrophe of repudiation, it is just a time shift. Repayment must eventually be made from funds obtained as a transferee in some capacity from the private sector with taxes the major transfer mechanism.[1]

But a significant supplement comes to the government as purveyor of various sorts of benefits – natural resources, goods, services, privileges. How to classify payment for things the law imposes on the payors deserves and will receive further consideration. One who seeks any of these for which a money charge is made pays not taxes but a price, whatever the formal terminology employed.[2] Sales of crown lands, fares on public transportation systems, university tuition fees, are familiar traditional illustrations of a range of instances expanding with the proliferation of crown corporations and other forms of government enterprise. Charges of this kind seldom pay the full cost of the service which must depend on additions made on grounds of public policy from true tax funds. Yet, substantial in the aggregate, their existence forbids equating tax receipts with what is available for meeting government expenses. To such items, constitutional provisions dealing with taxation have therefore no application. Their constitutional position rests instead on whether the benefits purchased are of a kind which it is for the grantor government to be supplying under its grants of substantive competence.[3]

Much more important than non-tax contributions to government supply are the non-income-generating aspects of taxation. These are of two orders. Measures enacted disguised as taxation may be tailored to burden and discourage disfavoured activities, with money really no object. Others may have fiscal consequences as the primary objective, not as providing the sinews of government but for controlling the general functioning of the economy. These radically different types call for separate comment.

Customs duties although taxes have been recognized alike in Canada,[4]

1 Borrowing can also be used as a control mechanism for the general level of economic activity; see infra, at 38–9.
2 See *A.-G. Can.* v *Toronto* (1893) 23 S.C.R. 514 (water rates); *Harper* v *State of Victoria* (1966) 114 C.L.R. 361, at 376 (per McTiernan J) (inspection and grading services); *City of Philadelphia* v *Holmes Electric Protection Co* (1939) 335 Pa. 273, 6 A. 2d 884 (private easement in street).
3 See Aubert, *Traité de droit constitutionelle suisse* II (1967), at 692, noting a distinction between *impôts* and *émoluments* and taxes along the lines suggested in the text.
4 *A.-G. B.C.* v *A.-G. Can.* [1924] A.C. 222

Australia,[5] and the United States[6] as being also laws for the regulation of foreign commerce, valid as such without falling afoul of constitutionally safeguarded provincial (state) tax immunity. What weight will be given the regulatory nature of a law cloaked as a tax is obscure in other contexts. There has been a disposition to condemn provincial[7] or state[8] measures of that kind as trespasses on areas of federal regulatory competence.[9] Where federal statutes purporting to be tax laws are involved the record is less clear. An early inclination to recognize the reality of impermissible regulation behind the mask of taxation seems to have been abandoned. Letting the federal government strike at conduct within its regulatory competence through a crippling tax rather than in some other way involves only a choice of means. But reliance on approval of that as authorizing wholesale disregard of the true thrust of the legislation slurs over that critical consideration. Precedent does not call for blindness to the statute's character nor does principle. The axiom that the motives of the legislature are political in character hence not proper for judicial examination, it has been argued, excludes any reference to effects and confines attention to the act's expressed command as the sole criterion of its nature.[10] The axiom one accepts. But motive is not the same as intent. While courts should refrain from querying the policies a legislature sees fit to pursue, they cannot, where a constitution specifies legislative competence, properly refrain from examining whether those policy choices relate to matters belonging to the enacting legislature. Discretion about how to act is not discretion about what to act upon. Court scrutiny of the former is improper, of the latter a duty.

All unpleasant consequences tend to discourage. Tax liability is an unpleasant consequence. Every situation which attracts a tax is to a degree discouraged. With some the discouragement bears no comparison with the attractiveness of the occasioning circumstance. Such include the receipt of income, the ownership of property or its taking as a gift or from a decedent. But, where the alternatives are less lopsided, the deterrent potential of the tax liability becomes important. Its relative weight is always the question. Only if on balance it is so burdensome that it may be assumed few will care to incur it should it be condemned as being some-

---

5   *A.-G. N.S.W.* v *Collector of Customs* (1908) 5 C.L.R. 818
6   *University of Illinois* v *United States* (1938) 289 U.S. 48
7   See *A.-G. Alta* v *A.-G. Can.* [1939] A.C. 117
8   See Powell, Business taxation and interstate commerce, in *Proceedings of the Thirtieth Annual Conference of the National Tax Association* (1938), at 337–59.
9   But cf. *Natal Land & Colonization Co* v *Commissioner of Taxes* (1910) 31 Natal L.R. 1 (provincial quadrupling of tax rates on land 'not beneficially occupied' sustained as exercise of provincial taxing power).
10 See Wynes, supra, chapter 2, note 50, at 38.

thing other than a tax. But, where it is, the gist of the legislation is repression rather than taxation. Perhaps as good a test as any is to ask whether, the less the revenue collected, the more the statute's purpose will have been attained. The tax then is only a means to an end. To allow the means to justify a forbidden end is to abdicate judicial responsibility to guard the constitutionally established allocation of regulatory authority, not an inquiry into motives or policy.

The proposed draft emphasizes at both the federal and the provincial levels that the taxing authority is to be used for money-raising and not for regulatory purposes. It does so by framing the power as one for 'the raising of money' in a particular way, namely, by taxation. Thus it departs from the Australian formula vesting parliament with the power of 'taxation' *simpliciter*.[11] It departs even more widely from the US constitution's bestowal of congressional power 'to lay and collect taxes ...' with its appendant 'to ... provide for the ... general welfare of the United States,'[12] a phrase whose long-argued ambiguity finally has been resolved in favour of using it as an opening for federal interposition in internal state policies. It conforms instead to the pattern in the BNA Act,[13] stressing the raising of revenue rather than just taxation. Its reiteration should jolt the courts out of the general neglect of that pattern.

This does not deny that appropriate regulation can be packaged in the form of a tax. It should however be recognized and appraised for its regulatory substance and not for its form. One can tax by taxing. One can regulate by taxing. Only the former is comprehended by this grant.

That is not a restriction to raising sums for meeting the expenses of government within the fields assigned. As appears elsewhere,[b] one main grant of law-making power to the central government is with respect to 'the structure and functioning of the economy.' Economists, while disagreeing about the independent efficacy and the mechanics of application of fiscal measures, are in general agreement that they are an important weapon in the arsenal of control over the general level of economic activity. Regarding inflation and depression as linked with the amount of funds available to the private sector, they see increases or decreases in them as influencing investment and spending decisions to the end of attaining or maintaining the level desired. Currency issue and the crea-

---

11 Section 55 ('Laws imposing taxation shall deal only with the imposition of taxation, and any provisions therein dealing with any other matter shall be of no effect'), apparently concerned with this problem, has been effectively eviscerated: see *Nott Bros & Co Ltd* v *Barkley* (1925) 36 C.L.R. 20; Wynes, supra, chapter 2, note 50, at 189.

12 Article 1, s 8, cl 1

13 Ss 91(3), 92(2)

b The proposal with respect to the federal power of economic regulation was to be developed in succeeding chapters. The grant of power is set out supra, at 5.

tion of public debt are ways of feeding funds into the private sector, taxes a way of withdrawing them from it. Use for that purpose is regulation indeed but regulation within a field of competence assigned to the federal government.

Admittedly withdrawal from the private sector will not occur if money is simply recycled through provincial expenditures to the private sector by the annual flow-through of all excess funds through the Canadian Equalization Council to the provinces.[14] But the council in its allocations may be expected to take into account not only the provinces' current costs of current operations but their burden of indebtedness on past borrowings. To the extent that tax receipts are used to repay and retire existing obligations of government, federal or provincial, they can be deflationary. Moreover, even used for current programs, diversion to regional pockets, where human or other resources are unemployed or underemployed for lack of purchasing power from those where the opposite situation exists, ought not to modify substantially the utility of the tax as a regulator of over-all Canadian economic activity. Deflationary consequences are not relevant where the private sector is already starved for funds. The operations of the council have primarily to do with spending not taxing and will be discussed more fully in that connection; but it does have a supporting role, which should be noted, in the use of taxes as a regulator of the level economic activity.

The point is that for any substantive power entrusted to parliament the federal government should be able to use taxes as an instrument of regulation – but not for anything left to the provinces. What is unique about its use in this context is that the aim is the raising of revenue, just as with true taxes, but raising it to shift resources from the private sector, not to provide for expenses. The provinces too may employ taxation as the operating mechanism within their range of regulatory competence.

So in what follows about the structuring of taxing power, it is not intended to foreclose inquiry into whether the taxing power is being exercised for permissible ends as elsewhere defined by the constitution. That is a preliminary requirement. The tax provisions are intended to operate in that setting.

A viable federal system demands that each level of government possess its own power to tax.

The central authority cannot have handouts. A major defect in the articles of confederation was felt to be the dependence of the Continental Congress on requisitions to the states to obtain supply. Even the European Economic Community has found it necessary to make a limited and timid

14 See infra, at 80–105.

beginning to authorizing taxation by the central body – without of course derogating from national authority to tax in any way not creating trade barriers between members.

Conversely where local taxing powers rest on statutory grant and not constitutional entitlement, the quality of discretionary use does not signify a federal relationship. Indeed delegation implies subordination and negates the non-hierarchical status of governments which is the essence of that relationship.[15] Municipalities and specialized local authorities have traditionally and commonly been vested with some measure of tax autonomy. So have the regional regimes sometimes established in unitary states as decentralizing adaptations responding to local situations and sentiments.[16] The source, not the existence or extent, of the authority is critical. It is fully consistent with the federal principle for one level to undertake to opt to stay out of an area of jointly possessed taxing authority,[17] but not for it to be subject to being put out.

Either may as part of the constitutional scheme be kept out of some of the taxable universe. In fact that is an ordinary feature of federal constitutions.

All of them speak to the power to tax. All vest a taxing power in the central parliament. With but a single exception[18] they undertake some specification of the extent of authority to tax. Beyond that there is no uniformity of prescription. The principles of some measure of reciprocal immunity from each other's taxes[19] and of shielding the flow of inter-provincial and foreign commerce from the barrier potential inherent in provincial taxation[20] are widely accepted; but in concrete expression they take different shapes, reflecting the different approaches to structuring the tax clauses in the constitutions.

Otherwise there is the utmost variety. The differences may, however, be classified into two types. One relates to the way the constitution expresses limitations on the taxing power, the other to what level of government it concerns itself with.

Limitations have been established sometimes by a formula, sometimes by a catalogue, or the two in combination. The formula technique stand-

15 *Hodge v The Queen* (1883) 9 App. Cas. 117
16 Eg, in Italy, where art 119 of the constitution provides that the regions may levy their own taxes.
17 As provided in the Canadian federal-provincial tax rental agreements; see infra, at 324.
18 The Communist bloc countries describing themselves as federations – the USSR and Yugoslavia – which use a different mechanism than taxation for apportioning resources between the union and republic governments
19 See infra, at 49–54.
20 See infra, at 45–7.

ing alone is employed in Canada,[21] the United States[22] and Argentina,[23] and is primarily relied on in Mexico.[24] The procedure of cataloguing particular objects of taxation is slightly commoner. Sometimes federal and provincial lists mutually exclusive are appended as schedules.[25] Rather more often the constitution embodies a specification of taxable matters exclusive or concurrent as the case may be.[26] Viewed as a group, the lists are a mixed bag. The items included, in response to special situations of time and place one may surmise, appear partly to reflect some judgment about access to adequate resources for the recipient government but usually, insofar as they involve excise taxes which they generally do, about the appropriate location of regulatory authority. In any event they form a jumble of particulars to which tax measures must conform to be valid. Some countries which catalogue also state supplemental principles; thus, in Brazil federal taxes must be uniform throughout the nation[27] and in Venezuela, progressive rates are to be a principle.[28] Australia is unique in expressing no limitations either categorical or descriptive on its grant of taxing authority.[29]

All deal with the federal taxing power. Ordinarily only it has attracted attention in those constitutions which define the characteristics of authorized taxes instead of setting out lists of taxable subjects.[30] Except for exclusions noted earlier[31] regarding reciprocal immunities and impediments to the free flow of trade, provincial taxing power is left implicit and its ambit at large. But all the constitutions which allocate tax subjects set

21 See the BNA Act, s 92(2)
22 See US Constitution, art 1, s 8, cl 1 ('All Duties, Imposts and Excises shall be uniform throughout the United States.'); art 1, s 9, cl 4 ('No capitation, or other direct tax shall be levied, unless in proportion to the Census or Enumeration hereinbefore directed to be taken.').
23 See Constitution of Argentina, art 67(2) (congress may levy 'direct taxes for a specified time and proportionately equal throughout the national territory, whenever the defense, security and the general welfare of the State so require').
24 See Constitution of Mexico, art 73 (VII) (congress may 'levy the taxes necessary to cover the budget'). To this is joined a power to tax foreign commerce, government concessions, and natural resources (art 73 (xxix)).
25 Eg, Constitution of India, Seventh Schedule; Federal Constitution of Malaysia, Ninth Schedule
26 See Constitution of Brazil, c v; Basic Law of the Federal Republic of Germany, art 105; Federal Constitution of the Swiss Confederation, passim; Constitution of the Republic of Venezuela, arts 17, 18, 136(8), 137.
27 Constitution of Brazil, art 20
28 Constitution of the Republic of Venezuela, art 223
29 Other than the requirement that they 'not ... discriminate between states or parts of states': Commonwealth of Australia Constitution Act, s 51(ii)
30 Those of Argentina, Australia, Mexico, and the United States
31 Supra, at 40.

bounds on what the member governments may tax, although Switzerland does so only by forbidding them to tax any of the range of subjects mentioned in article 41A.

Canada is exceptional. While the BNA Act employs a formula and not a list, its constraint applies only to the provinces whose taxes must be 'direct ... within the Province in order to the raising of a Revenue for Provincial Purposes'[32] while parliament may 'rais[e] money by any mode or system of Taxation.'[33] In thus exposing provincial but not federal taxes to challenge as improper in kind, it goes beyond even those regimes which distribute fields of taxation between the two levels[34] and still further beyond all those which like it undertake a generic limitation.

Although the existence of its own taxing authority for each level is critical for federalism, a constitution goes far enough when it creates it for the common government and recognizes it either implicitly or still better by express confirmation for the members. The statement in any way of limitations, beyond those inherent in its really being a tax and in its not impinging on the functioning of the system to achieve a common purpose, only invites confusion and, in countries where statutes must survive judicial scrutiny for constitutionality, litigation. Regulatory powers without fixed boundaries would expose the citizen to a call for compliance with discordant directives or at the very least to wasteful duplication of enforcement programs; tax overlaps have no such consequence. If different authorities elect to tax an identical subject the 'taxes may co-exist and be enforced without clashing'[35] each reaping its part of the taxpayer's holdings without getting in the other's way.

Attempts to parcel out the fields have all resulted in either piecemeal reallocation or a mishmash of court interpretations.

The former has characterized constitutions which use the listing procedure. Central governments that are authorized to shift items out of the provincial list by legislative or constituent action[36] use that power freely to whittle down inconvenient reservations to the provinces, at times 'in a more or less casual manner without reference to the Cabinets or legislatures of the States concerned.'[37]

32 S 92(2)
33 S 91(3)
34 Some constitutions, eg those of Brazil (c v) and India (art. 248(2)), extend the federal taxing authority to any field not specified, but even they leave it open to question a federal law on the ground that it falls within the provincial list.
35 See the remarks of Lord Macmillan in *Forbes* v *A.-G. Man.* [1937] A.C. 260, at 274.
36 Constitution of Austria, art 14; Basic Law of the Federal Republic of Germany, art 105; Constitution of India, art 368 (by which parliament is made the constitutional amending organ)
37 Lanthanam, The changing pattern of union-state relations in India, (1963), 9 *Indian J. Pub. Admin.* 457, at 462. Easy resort to this device may run counter to public sentiment,

In those countries using descriptive formulas, what has happened is only exceptionally a dismantling of the restrictions.[38] Normally, a decisional cloud has developed around the terms employed whose nice – or whimsical, as one chooses – distinctions baffle easy comprehension. The classic example is the directness limitation under section 92(2) of the BNA Act, a provision which presents other difficulties of interpretation as well.[39] The refinement which forbids sales taxes while accepting their Siamese twin, use taxes, exalts form over substance. Value-added taxes are clearly out of bounds under the formula – but why should a province not be allowed to choose that method of taxing?

Two explanations suggest themselves, although none has to my knowledge been articulated, for so complicating the powers to tax with qualifications on its exercise. Both are misconceived attempts to deal with things functionally associated with but not an integral element of taxation. More sensitive than the courts to tax incidence as an instrument for stimulating or discouraging activity, the constitutional texts undertake a generally similar division of tax and of regulatory competence between the levels. That is more conspicuously the case where lists are sent out. They tend to specify for the provinces matters with a strong local flavour and for the federal authority those impinging on unified policy. Indeed there is a trace of this in the treatment of customs duties. Universally they are reserved to parliament – even in Australia[40] where the tax power is otherwise unqualified. Once the choice is made which matters fall within which level's appropriate domain it is natural enough to seek to secure that level's quiet enjoyment of the field. The awkward indirectness of tax lumping is, however, ill-suited to that end. The proper approach is a realistic distinction of true taxes from regulatory measures wearing a tax mask. The latter should be sustained only if within the regulatory competence of the enacting government. True taxes on the other hand almost by definition will have no chilling effect on conduct. Their utility as

as evidenced by the Swiss experience. There, where constitutional amendments must be approved by referendum, sweeping transfers out of the cantonal list have twice been rejected: see Aubert, supra, chapter 2, note 3, at 283–6.

38 The most notable example is amendment XVI to the US Constitution, overcoming the decision in *Pollock* v *Farmers Loan & Trust Co* (1845) 157 U.S. 429, that the federal income tax involved there was a direct tax and, not being apportioned among the states, was unconstitutional.

39 The materials will be found in *Laskin's Canadian Constitutional Law*, supra, chapter 2, note 34, at 643–99. Identical language used in South Africa to define the taxing powers of provincial councils (see Union of South Africa Act 1909, s 85(i)) has been applied in an apparently contrary sense to that accepted in Canada (see *Comm'r for Inland Revenue* v *Royal Exchange Assurance Co* [1925] A.D. 222; *Clarke & Co* v *De Waal N.O.* [1922] A.D. 264), although both countries purport to accept John Stuart Mill's test of directness as primary.

40 Commonwealth of Australia Constitution Act, s 90

revenue sources presupposes that the taxed activity continues to flourish. Classification which echoes regulatory considerations is beside the mark for pure money-gathering measures. It serves only to impose artificial rigidities frustrating and teasing normally resources-hungry governments.

The other plausible explanation of the restrictions placed on taxes is the circumstance that they are the prime means for financing the operations of government. With spending following getting, they are thought of as reciprocals. It is widely accepted, particularly in countries like Canada and the United States which used formula limitations, that the constitutional framers sought to estimate the amounts that would be needed for each level to meet its assigned responsibilities and to provide it with tax (and other) resources adequate for that purpose. This overlooked the non-revenue raising uses of taxation. More importantly, it projected both expenses and tax yields on the assumed continuance of conditions existing at the time the constitution was framed. But both have changed and are bound to change in unforeseeable ways. With spending just as with regulatory authority, effective constitutional controls need to address themselves to the issue direct rather than treating it as a side effect of tax competence.

It is therefore proposed to unfetter the taxing power recognized as belonging to both the federation and the members on the same general basis.[41] The broad range allowed the dominion under the BNA Act should be open to the provinces save for customs duties. The language suggested is modelled on that now found in section 91(3). The position would then in effect be the same as that in Australia. A difference in the phraseology proposed emphasizes, however, that the provisions authorize only true

41 Cf *Final Report of the Special Joint Committee of the Senate and the House of Commons on the Constitution of Canada* (1972), at 48:

RECOMMENDATIONS

54 Generally speaking and subject to recommendation 55 we endorse the principle that the Federal and Provincial Governments should have access to all fields of taxation. However, in order to bring about a division of revenues that may accurately reflect the priorities of each government, there should be Federal-Provincial consultations to determine the most equitable means of apportioning joint fields of taxation in the light of:

A the projected responsibilities of each level of government in the immediate future;

B the anticipated increases in their respective expenditures;

C economic and administrative limitations, such as preserving sufficient leverage for the Federal Government, by means of its taxation system, to discharge effectively its function of managing the economy.

55 Provincial Legislatures should have the right to impose indirect taxes provided that they do not impede interprovincial or international trade and do not fall on persons resident in other Provinces. These limitations could be satisfied by tax collection through an interprovincial or Federal Provincial collection agency, or by tax collection agreements.

tax measures as distinguished from regulatory legislation which must find its justification in other grants. Where Australia vests parliament with the power of 'taxation,' the proposed draft stresses 'the raising of revenue,' with taxation a subsidiary means to that end. In so doing, it only repeats the terms of section 91(3). True, they have been ignored. Blindness to them ought not to be repeated. There is no more excuse for erasing them by inattention than for bypassing any other provision of the constitution. Given the weight which they invite, they direct attention to the requirement that only genuine tax legislation can pass muster under these grants.

Confinement of the tax power to its proper content does not eliminate the need for serious attention to the matters to which it has been instrumental – regulation and spending. For the former, that calls only for circumspection in recognizing a *détournement de pouvoir* and in determining, if regulation is indeed involved, to what legislature the relevant regulatory competence belongs. For the latter special arrangements must be designed to replace the haphazard empirical practices that have developed in the absence of clear definition. Before entering on a consideration of such arrangements, however, let me deal with a brace of limitations on the taxing power itself which it seems desirable to retain.

As was noted earlier, all existing federations confine the imposition of duties on imports to the federal legislative to the exclusion of the members. In those which follow the listing technique this is done by their mention in the federal list[42] or by hiving them off from a concurrent list in an exclusive federal list.[43] In those which leave tax fields generally or provincial tax fields specifically unlisted, the same result is attained by provisions variously formulated which predicate the existence of federal and negative provincial authority.

Inter se exactions of a like character are also forbidden. Their dual fiscal and commercial nature has led to treating the prohibition sometimes in connection with the taxing sections of the constitution[44] and sometimes from the viewpoint of internal freedom of trade.[45] Australia with its requirement that '[o]n the imposition of uniform duties of customs, trade,

42 Eg, Basic Law of the Federal Republic of Germany, art 73
43 Eg, BNA Act, s 122; Commonwealth of Australia Constitution Act, ss 86, 90; Constitution of Mexico, arts 73 (XXIX), 117; US Constitution, art 1, s 8, cl 1, s 10, cl 2 (such duties not to be laid 'without the consent of Congress,' which has not in practice been given, and to be subject to 'the Revision and Control of the Congress'; amendment XXI has however apparently removed the constraints in the one instance of importation of intoxicating liquors: see *State Board of Equalization* v *Young's Market Co* (1936) 299 U.S. 59.)
44 Eg, Constitution of Mexico, art 117; Constitution of Argentina, arts 108, 67(1)
45 In Switzerland the immunity from such taxes would seem more properly to be based on art 31, stipulating freedom of trade throughout the Confederation except as authorized by the Federal Constitution, than on art 28 making customs a federal matter.

commerce, and intercourse among the States ... shall be absolutely free'[46] and Canada, in providing that '[a]ll Articles of the Growth, Produce or Manufacture of any one of the Provinces shall ... be admitted free into each of the other Provinces'[47] take the latter approach. In the United States, the text of the constitution says nothing explicitly to the point, what with the Supreme Court's shrinkage of 'imports' in article 1, clause 10, to mean only goods brought in from outside.[48] Nevertheless, '[i]mports and duties are placed beyond the power of a state, without the mention of an exception, by the provision committing commerce of that order to the powers of the Congress.'[49] All three congruent confederations thus focus on the free flow of internal trade rather than on customs being a species of tax.

Their inherent operation as trade barriers dictates the existence and extent of the limits on the availability of international and interprovincial customs duties.

To allow the provinces to exact either would be to create a loophole for regulating commercial activity which it is generally accepted should be immune from their control. The reasons for immunity are not quite the same for interprovincial as for international commerce.

A necessary quality of even the most pallid confederation is equal receptiveness by each member to goods coming from any other as for local ones. Indeed still looser associations sometimes have that objective. The European Economic Community, herein suggested with some additions as the general blueprint for a new constitution, has as a leading principle 'the elimination as between Member States of customs duties and of quantitative restrictions in regard to the importation and exportation of goods, as well as all other measures with equivalent effect.'[50] They were prohibited[51] with a grace period for their elimination which was in fact accelerated by the member states.[52]

A blend of economic and political considerations supports free movement between members. From the economic point of view, a major inducement for coming together is the belief that an enlarged market will benefit both sellers and buyers, the one by making possible economies of scale and more efficient investment decisions, the other by the benefits to be expected from the increase in competing suppliers. Politically, provincially imposed exactions would lead to friction and retaliation, federal ones could fairly be seen as cheating the members of a principal material

46 Commonwealth of Australia Constitution Act, s 92
47 BNA Act, s 121
48 See *Hooven & Allison Co* v *Evatt* (1945) 324 U.S. 652.
49 See *Baldwin* v *G.A.F. Seelig Inc* (1935) 294 U.S. 511, at 522.
50 Treaty Establishing the European Economic Community, art 3(a)
51 Ibid, art 9
52 See Matheson, *A Guide to European Community Law* (1972), at 38–9.

benefit expected from association. For either level to tax the movement of goods between members would disrupt the common commitment to market reciprocity. The United States by narrowly reading 'imports' has perhaps opened the way for federal internal customs duties (without so far travelling it); if it is the commerce clause that constrains the states, the reference of internal customs to it rather than to taxation suggests that the uniformity limitation established for federal indirect taxation has no bearing and hence exposes the states to the discrimination possible in the plenary discretion under the commerce clause.[53] Congress, it may be said, would never do it; but many measures long supposed to be just as alien to congressional decision have been adopted and sustained. By their provisions foreclosing any such possibility, Australia and Canada have acted prudently. That should continue. The Australian formula is preferable. It condemns barriers to both entry and exit while Canada deals only with free admission.

Foreign commerce is different. Here too customs duties are entangled with commercial regulation. However, unlike internal customs they do not prejudice the access of the production of any province to the market in any other province, with the consequent risk of domestic discord. Whatever the level, protection will operate only against foreigners. Any advantage will extend equally to the same produce of all provinces. The reasons for forbidding internal customs therefore do not apply. Rather the vice lies in breaching the necessarily unitary control of the central government over external relations. That requirement which dictates withholding power from the provinces permits and even presumes its existence in parliament. Clearly it may be and visibly has been exercised so as to produce or aggravate regional economic disparities. But commercial regulation generally, not just the tariff, has been misused thus. The perils and the benefits of federal control attach to all alike. The critical feature of import duties is their function as a bargaining chip in external affairs. The considerations that support giving competence there to parliament intersect with those assigning trade regulation to it. Federal systems without exception reflect this. They all vest in the central legislature authority here while denying it to the members and usually denying to both authority to subject interprovincial transactions to customs duties. No departure from that widely accepted pattern is proposed. However, a special provision, elsewhere set out,[54] undertakes to cancel to some degree the capacity of customs duties for prejudicing provinces or regions.

Export duties are not the mirror image they seem to be. Addressed to

---

53 Cf *New England Divisions Case* (1923), 261 U.S. 184.
54 See the discussion of the role of the Canadian Equalization Council, infra, at 338–63. The proceeds of customs duties would form part of a fund for distribution to the provinces.

goods moving out of the country, they do, like import duties, implicate both external affairs and commercial regulation.

Federal competence would seem proper just as it is for the latter. Indeed it is sometimes expressly recognized.[55] The United States, however, in terms forbids them.[56] Neither Australia nor Canada does. With economies largely dependent as both have been on exportation of primary products, neither has seen much occasion to discourage it by imposing them. In principle, parliament's power seems to rest here on the same grounds as that over import duties. The capacity for selective application prejudicing a province or region which led to the US prohibition[57] clearly exists but the two are just alike in that respect. The US example, withdrawing one option for regulating international trade in one special way, is an aberration which should not be followed.

Should provincial export duties be permitted? Applicable only to things moving out of Canada, what with the constitutional guarantee of interprovincial free trade, they would not threaten harmonious relations between the members. Still they would have elements of regulation of external commerce, something which is not a provincial function. That would likely be only a side effect. The primary objective would be stimulation of domestic enterprise by establishing a split-level price scale for local resources.[58] With industrial development and the incident increase of employment opportunity a proper subject for provincial action, export duties designed to that end, while they would be, as argued earlier, regulatory and not truly fiscal measures, would be regulations of a matter within provincial competence. Viewed formally as taxes, they like other taxes should be equally available to the provinces and the central government. Viewed substantially as regulations, they would embody policies validly provincial. In contrast with customs on imports, as to which discouragement of external trade is the critical prerequisite and domestic impact a collateral contingent hope, export duties are only auxiliary to the achievement of an internal program, which would be pursued without them but which they may be thought to further. The proposed restriction on the provinces is therefore confined to customs on imports only.

This represents a clear departure from existing practice. The US constitution forbids state duties without congressional assent and even then subject to qualifications on a parity for import and export, except that the

55 Eg, Constitution of Mexico, art 73 (xxix); Federal Constitution of the Swiss Confederation, art 28; Constitution of India, schedule 7, list 1, item 83.
56 US constitution, art 1, s 9, cl 5 ('No Tax or Duty shall be laid on Articles exported from any State.')
57 See Rawle, *A View of the Constitution of the United States of America* (2d ed 1829), at 115–16.
58 Because of the interprovincial free trade guarantee, the more favourable terms would be available to industry wherever located in Canada.

latter are permitted for those 'absolutely necessary for executing inspection laws.'[59] Australia speaks more obliquely, making 'the power of Parliament to impose duties of customs ... exclusive.'[60] In Canada, a textual basis is wholly lacking unless a hint of one is to be found in transitional permissions;[61] but the limitation to 'direct taxation' has been invoked to ban such duties.[62] The practice seems to reflect only an undeliberated assimilation of import and export duties. It should be discarded, given the difference between them.

Admittedly, provincial export duties would impinge on external commerce. Regulation of that is for the central, not the member governments. This creates no real dilemma with the assumed continuance of the constitutional principles now familiar as the aspect doctrine and, modified in a manner not here relevant, paramountcy. As measures for the promotion of industrial activity, they would be within provincial legislative competence. Yet parliament could make whatever laws about external commerce it chooses and risks no loss of its options in dealing with international relations. Any laws made by parliament would, on paramountcy principles, suspend the operation of incompatible provincial measures. If none are made, why should provincial discretion be curtailed?

The accommodations needed to respect the status of non-hierarchical authorities present in the same territory occur in many contexts. Even in the tax area, they are not confined to the components of federations. There are analogies for instance, in medieval church-state relations[63] and in the rules of international law about state-owned property.

The root sentiments there operative probably support its having been taken for granted that some measure of reciprocal tax immunity be extended. There seems to have been no systematic exposition of the reasons. Perhaps the minor amounts initially involved relative to the total available tax sources made the costs of concession seem less than those of maintaining a bone of contention between fairly matched power centres which had to coexist. Between monarchs of newly emerging nation states, feelings of professional courtesy may have combined with recognizing the possibility of a return in kind to establish diplomatic practice. When federal states came to be formed and their constitutions written, these

---

59 Art I, s 10, cl 2
60 Commonwealth of Australia Constitution Act, s 90. 'Customs duty' is said to be 'a duty on ... importation or exportation'; see the *Petrol Case* (1926) 38 C.L.R. 408, at 435 (per Higgins J), 438 (per Starke J).
61 See BNA Act, ss 122–4, all long since spent.
62 See *Texada Mines v A.-G. B.C.* [1960] S.C.R. 713
63 For a discussion of medieval church-state relations, see Gardiner, *Constitutional Documents of the Puritan Revolution 1625–1660* (3d ed 1906).

older natural and rational patterns which had evolved independently were taken over without extended discussion.

The theory of dual sovereignty on which the US constitution was based would suggest that the states and the union each treat the other much as either would treat any outside sovereign.[64] In Canada and Australia, the crown remained the single sovereign but the freedom from local taxation which inhered to it before the conferring of dominion status continued as a crown attribute at each level. In each case history supplies the reasonable justification which nobody bothered to articulate. The best argument for a modicum of abstention, it may be argued, is precisely the fact that it has encountered no argument.

Canada and Australia wrote the principle into their constitutions. The phrasing differs slightly. In the former, 'No Lands or Property belonging to Canada or to any Province shall be liable to Taxation.'[65] In the latter, 'A State shall not, without the consent of the Parliament of the Commonwealth ... impose any tax of any kind on property belonging to the Commonwealth nor shall the Commonwealth impose any tax on property belonging to a State.'[66]

The US constitution is silent on the point. The articles of confederation had provided that 'no imposition, duties or restriction shall be laid by any state, on the property of the United States or either of them'[67] and, with the Continental Congress having no power to tax, the exemption was effectively reciprocal. There was no equivalent in the successor constitution. Nor was the dropping of it put in issue. It was not an item in any of the numerous accompanying proposals for amendment made in connection with state ratifications. Judicial construction restored the immunity of federal property from state taxes.[68] The converse has never come up for decision. Because of the impracticability of apportionment, required for direct taxes, there has been no federal property taxation. There are dicta intimating that, should the occasion arise, state property could not be subjected to it.[69]

Yet neither the textual nor the doctrinal shields protect fully against taxation by the other level.

They affect only property taxation. Their scope is thus more limited than that of some other federal constitutions, such as the Brazilian provision that 'The Union, the States, and the Municipalities are forbidden ...

---

64 See *New York* v *U.S.* (1946) 326 U.S. 572, at 587 (per Stone CJ), 594–5 (per Douglas J).
65 BNA Act, s 125
66 Commonwealth of Australia Constitution Act, s 114
67 Art IV, cl 1
68 *Clallam County* v *U.S.* (1923) 263 U.S. 341; *Van Brocklin* v *Tennessee* (1886) 117 U.S. 151
69 *New York* v *U.S.*, supra note 64.

(*c*) to tax income, goods or services of each other.'[70] The special situation of customs duties, demandable from states or provinces not as taxes but as commercial regulations, has been noted.[71] Sales and use taxes where a government is the seller or user, death duties on bequests to it, stamp duties on conveyances by or to it, levies imposed on activity involved in its execution of the laws, income taxes on government businesses have invited claims to exemption. Clearly none comes within the general understanding of a property tax. In the United States, an abundant jurisprudence has sheltered the federal government from most[72] but not all[73] such state taxes but has subjected the states to most[74] but not all[75] similar federal taxes. The meagre Australian authority holding states liable to a federal payroll tax[76] and the commonwealth to a state stamp duty on land transfers[77] seems more to equate the position of the two levels. No Canadian authority squarely in point has been discovered.[78]

The significance of the textual shield for property is probably not so much the immunization of property it directly decrees as its grounding negative implication as to other taxes. The considerations that induce the widespread exemption of property of religious and eleemosynary organizations, fortified by those noted as arising from the concepts of dual sovereignty and of succession to the imperial crown, could have been expected to relieve the property owned by each level of the burden of taxation as they have in fact relieved it with or without mention. The value of property publicly owned moreover is a small fraction of the aggregate of property values. In situations where it is significant, the governmental owner often relinquishes its favoured position by agreeing to compensatory payments. In recognizing the special status of such property, there is no important impairment of the tax base.

That is less true of some of the other forms of taxation. With the

---

70 Art 32
71 Supra, notes 4–6 and accompanying text
72 See Schwartz, *American Constitutional Law* (1955), at 179–81.
73 States may impose inheritance taxes upon bequests to the federal government: *U.S. v Perkins* (1896) 163 U.S. 625.
74 Eg, *New York v U.S.*, supra note 24; *South Carolina v U.S.* (1905) 109 U.S. 437
75 *Ambrossini v U.S.* (1902) 187 U.S. 1
76 *Victoria v The Commonwealth* (1971) 122 C.L.R. 353
77 *The Commonwealth v New South Wales* (1918) 25 C.L.R. 325; but cf *Re Gardner* (1919) 15 Tas. L.R. 78 (commonwealth not liable to state probate duty on bequest).
78 *R. v Bell Telephone Co.* (1935) 59 Que. K.B. 205, the most relevant case, sustained the company's recovery from the province of Quebec of amounts paid by the company under the federal Special War Revenue Act, which imposed a tax on long-distance telephone calls, to be paid by the company and recouped from its customers by adding the amount of the tax to their bills. The justices treated the claim for repayment as an authorized tariff item and not as a tax claim by the company, with only one judge dealing in passing with the operation of s 125.

increased volume of government borrowings, tax exemption of their obligations is being challenged by economists as distorting investment decisions and by non-economists as a tax escape valve for wealth. The spread of government activity into businesses formerly left to private enterprise diverts income flows which would have been exposed to income taxation. The historic pattern of tax exemption is not directly relevant to either case. The search for new revenue sources leads to analogizing these important items to comparable ones in the private sector with which they compete.

No clear principle has yet emerged. What vague indications there are rather suggest that the presence of an express exempting clause decreases the range of exemption outside the property context.

In the United States, where the constitution is silent and all depends on implication, the notion grows that federal taxation spares state activities as a matter of legislative grace rather than of constitutional compulsion. That the converse is not true is based on the inadequate ground of paramountcy – inadequate in that paramountcy operates as regards regulatory and not fiscal measures. As with foreign sovereign immunity, the law seems to be groping toward a necessarily nebulous distinction between functions properly governmental and those of an entrepreneurial character, with the implied immunity of states from federal taxes confined to the former.

In Australia's leading case,[79] different emphases by different justices spawned a litter of statements which are all in accord but do not greatly enlighten. The tax there in issue not being a property tax was not in violation of any 'express provision' of the constitution[80] and the general proposition that the states have a constitutional protection against the exercise of the taxing power cannot be accepted.[81] On the other hand, 'section 114 is not an exhaustive statement of the protection' of one level from another's taxes;[82] there is room for constitutional implication of other exemptions.[83] A commonwealth tax on the revenue of a state was proposed as within the implied immunity.[84] More generally, a criterion was mentioned, reminiscent of though perhaps somewhat weaker than the US view of exemption for the state's essential functions,[85] not unlike the Canadian doctrine guarding dominion companies against sterilization

79 *Victoria v The Commonwealth*, supra note 76
80 Ibid, at 369 (per Barwick CJ)
81 Ibid, at 409 (per Walsh J)
82 Ibid, at 393 (per Menzies J)
83 Ibid, at 404 (per Windeyer J)
84 Ibid
85 Ibid, at 392–3 (per Menzies J) (laws which 'operate to interfere with the performance by the State of its constitutional functions')

or destruction of their powers and capacities[86] which was indeed expressly adduced as an analogy.[87] All that can safely be concluded is that the Australian clause has left room for implication of some additional immunity but an immunity certainly no broader and perhaps somewhat narrower than that existing under the silent US constitution.

Finally, in Canada, there is only the obiter observation, 'il y a une exception toutefois. C'est celle de l'article 125 ... mais cette exception même implique à mon sens le droit reciproque de taxer par ailleurs la Couronne.'[88]

If mention of exemption has any effect, it seems to restrict its range, a result consistent with the underlying logic of *expressio unius*. Such possibility of further implication as the commonwealth opinions admit seems surely no broader and maybe a bit narrower than that under the hazy US judicial construct. It would no doubt be possible to incorporate a blanket reciprocal immunity. But that would be imprudent if investment tax shelters are to be avoided or sprawling government entrepreneurship is apprehended. The insertion of an express provision seems desirable, with the hope that it would operate in the manner suggested in Australia.

With government property and only government property exempt from taxation, a preliminary question will always be which government's rules shall govern the determination of whether the kind of relation existing with the assessed parcel shall be classified as a property interest. Under present Canadian law, 'property (and civil rights)' is generally a matter for provincial qualification.[89] 'The Public (i.e. federal) (Debt and) Property' is however an exception.[90] Except for money disbursements, no change in this respect is proposed. Hence in the first instance the federal government and the provinces would each decide that question by its own rules and through its own organs. Any challenge to that decision would go to the tribunal created to deal with jurisdictional conflicts between the two levels of government.

A difference between the Australian and the Canadian provisions calls for comment. Under the former, only cross-level property taxation is forbidden. Under the latter, the exempt quality inheres in the property. Thus taxation by sibling states or provinces comes within the Canadian but not the Australian ban. The United States, where the whole matter rests on implication, echoes Australia in holding property of one state which is located in another taxable by the latter.

86 See *Great West Saddlery Co* v *The King* [1921] 2 A.C. 91
87 *Victoria* v *The Commonwealth*, supra note 76, at 398 (per Windeyer J)
88 *R* v *Bell Telephone Co*, supra note 78, at 210 (per Letourneau J)
89 But cf *Johnson* v *A.-G. Alta* [1945] S.C.R. 127.
90 See *Laskin's Canadian Constitutional Law*, supra, chapter 2, note 34, at 484.

The Canadian policy is the sounder. The other by discriminating implies that the autonomous status of the central government is of greater dignity than that of the members. Their functions do differ in line with the constitutional allocation but it warps attitudes toward their relative positions to draw from that the conclusion that their qualified sovereignty is of any different order. Moreover interstate exemption by eliminating a potential for disputes and irritation contributes to the harmonious interaction required for a happy marriage. One member's property holdings in another and hence the taxes foregone will seldom be great. In any event the province of situs by its mastery of who can take property within its borders and on what terms can condition acquisition upon advance agreements for compensatory transfer payments like those currently authorized to municipalities.[91] Weighed against the demeaning imputation involved and the risk of friction, the sums involved do not warrant treating fellow members differently from the federal government for provincial property tax purposes.

91 Municipal Grants Act, R.S.C. 1970, C M-15

PROPOSED PROVISION

Federal moneys may be used for carrying out laws in effectuation of the
powers granted to or recognized in the federal government by this Constitution and otherwise only as directed by the Canadian Equalization
Council except with the unanimous concurrence of the provinces.

The draft proposal and the discussion that follows deal only with federal
spending. Issues raised by provincial spending are almost wholly political,
seldom constitutional. Prescribed appropriation procedures must be followed and specific prohibitions on use respected but those are the only
constraints. In particular, the expenditure of state or provincial money in
furtherance of action in matters of federal regulatory competence has
gone unchallenged, perhaps because in practice the members only exceptionally have had either the excess funds or the inclination for it. My
proposal provides as to them only in giving them the broad residual
power. That is enabling, not restrictive. The appropriate place for any
limitations on them is the provincial constitutions. Federal spending has
been the practical and is the present concern.

1 The costs of performing the functions by law assigned to any government must be met from the funds available to it.
2 In every federation, indeed in every good-sized social collectivity, there
   will be disparities, not necessarily constant in incidence, in the material
   resources of the members. That cannot be avoided. Nor can they be
   eliminated. But they can be alleviated.
3 Moreover, at the time governments join they often assert claims tend-
   ing to distribute existing debt burdens undertaken in reliance on revenue sources surrendered to the newly established government.
4 The organs as well as the debts of the associating units may have been
   created in reliance and depend for support on the relinquished resources until new ones are developed.
5 Crises which shatter the normal economic environment and can be
   countered only by departures from routine practices are certain to
   occur although at unpredictable times and in unpredictable forms.

The first two items are constants, calling for ongoing provision. The third and fourth, start-up conditions, and the fifth, episodic in character, properly operate only while what occasioned them continues. The deliberated compromises of constitution makers have addressed themselves extensively to the first four. The fifth, less often, has been supplied as an unstated premise by legitimating its invocation under existing circumstances.

They have all been treated as proper components in government spending. Because the principal, although not the only source of what there is to spend is taxation, consideration of them was often joined with consideration of the taxing power. The deliberations generally shaped the latter on the supposition that the provision thereby made would enable the taxing government to take care of the components listed above.

It has not worked out so. Generality of expression in the grant of the spending power left its operation to the attitudinal biases of judicial expounders. Emergence of new types of taxes and increased return from taxes old and new arising from the industrial expansion in important federal states have between them enlarged the revenues of central governments enormously, giving a surplus available for discretionary disbursements quite independent of the components noted. With a permissive judiciary, parliaments have yielded to the temptation to use money at hand beyond those bounds, to purchase acquiescence in policies not constitutionally theirs to formulate. Necessitous provinces are, like necessitous men, unfree. The consequence has been a steady erosion in favour of the central government of control over the effective regulation of fields of competence.

The outcome has been the same everywhere. The outset has been different almost everywhere. Each federation has tried its own way to tie the spending power down. None has worked. Examination of these various efforts and of their frustration can reveal their deficiencies and suggest how the proposal here made would correct them.

The federations to which these remarks apply and whose experience it seems relevant to examine are Australia, Canada, the Federal Republic of Germany, Switzerland, and the United States. The republics of the Marxist ones, the Soviet Union and Yugoslavia, more closely resemble profit centres in a vast industrial enterprise than they do their nominal congeners in the western world; because of that and their hierarchical parties' directive roles, they are not comparable. Brazil, Mexico, Venezuela, and India specify transfer of a part of the federal revenue to provinces (and municipalities); but the responsibilities entrusted to the latter are relatively low level, restricted even on paper and still more so in practice. Little would be gained by studying them even were there materials readily available.

Attention to the complex of problems involved in government spending grew with the passage of time. The later the constitution, the more comprehensive and intricate are its relevant provisions.

In 1787, the US constitution spoke only tangentially, in the clause authorizing congress 'to lay and collect taxes ... to pay the debts and Provide for the common Defense and general Welfare of the United States.'[1] The BNA Act 1867 was equally delphic in empowering parliament to make laws on matters coming within the class of subjects, 'The Public Debt and Property,'[2] but did add special arrangements regarding the antecedent debts of the colonies now becoming provinces and a tabular-formular commitment to annual grants to each of the provinces. The almost contemporaneous Swiss constitution of 1874, being a revision of an earlier one, consistent with the older pattern was relatively inexplicit; it did however, expressly set aside for the cantons a share in one federal tax,[3] a technique its amendments repeated from time to time.

In 1900 the Australian constitution directed the commonwealth takeover of 'current obligations of the State in respect of the departments transferred' and further authorized parliament to take over all or a proportion of state debts generally, subject to adjusting credits against state claims to surplus revenue.[4] The claims would arise under another clause whereby 'Parliament may provide, on such basis as it deems fair, for the monthly payment to the several States of all surplus revenue of the Commonwealth.'[5] That *carte blanche* was duplicated by empowering parliament for '10 years after the establishment of the Commonwealth and thereafter until the Parliament otherwise provides ... [to] grant financial assistance to the States on such terms and conditions as the Parliament sees fit.'[6] The Canadian attempt to work out a detailed settlement of accounts between those entering into partnership was thus abandoned in favour of broad parliamentary discretion to deal equitably with the dislocation of state finances occasioned by federation.

Germany in 1949 devised a highly sophisticated scheme. As was noted[7] tax sources there are assigned by category. The federal government and the länder (also municipalities) respectively are entitled to the revenue from those tax fields which are exclusively theirs. That from shared fields, and they are the most important, is divided between them on a basis fixed by the constitution but subject to revision by prescribed procedures. An

1 Art I, s 8, cl 1
2 91(1) (renumbered s 91(1A) by the BNA (No. 2) Act, 1949, 13 Geog. VI, c 81 (U.K.))
3 Art 41 bis, s 1, cl a
4 S 85(iv)
5 S 105
6 S 94
7 Supra, chapter 3, note 26

innovation is that, besides the federal-land participation in the shared taxes, a mechanism is established for sharing between states. Under it, those with a stronger tax base and consequent greater yields transfer some of their receipts to those less favourably situated. That indeed is the main equalizing agency. There are also federal subventions for that purpose as well as to assist in promoting activities of special types; but they are of less magnitude.

The progressive sophistication suggests growing sensitiveness to the central-member considerations involved in the disbursement of public money. The diversity of treatments shows how hard it is to frame a satisfactory subvention program. The existence of federal funds excess to federal functions is a precondition. They have derived from various sources – the sale of public lands, federal borrowings, but ordinarily from taxation.

In Switzerland and the United States it seems not to have been anticipated that federal taxes would bring in much more than enough to cover federal expenses. Nor did they for many years. But in both countries the opening up by constitutional amendment of immensely productive new tax sources changed that. In Canada and Australia, import duties had been the mainstay of colonial budgets prior to confederation. They were expected to be productive enough to take care of federal expenses, forecast in Australia as modest, and to leave substantial amounts over to apply to those of the provinces, forecast as modest in Canada. Under the German scheme, by which a fraction of the shared tax was set aside for each level without regard to the state of the federal treasury, the question of a surplus was irrelevant.

Both for allocating fields of tax competence and for dealing with any imbalance of income that might result, estimates of the return from the revenue sources and of the operating requirements of each level respective were commonly felt to be in order. With nothing to go on but past experience (under other circumstances) with the classes of taxes being federalized and the necessarily conjectural cost of governments either wholly new or with radically remodelled functions, constitution makers had no firm basis for either estimate. Yet they assumed that they could and should proceed to marry these two fetuses. The familiar recent past was their natural guide. Its vice was insufficient recognition that the future is always unpredictably different.

The succession everywhere of constitutional amendments, legislative circumventions, or judicial changes of tack is witness to the inherent obsolescence of any formula specified in advance. Only an ambulatory prescription for sharing funds can long be serviceable.

None of the five spending objectives noted at the beginning of this chapter involves a curtailment of recipient discretion as to the use of transferred funds.

Use to defray the cost of a government's own instrumentalities in the execution of its proper functions simply involves no transfer payments. Its propriety seems never to have been disputed. It is implied in the very grant of taxing authority.[8] The choice of it rather than a system of requisitions clearly means that the government may provide for its own support.

The draft expressly confirms this. In so doing, it specifies the effectuation of federal powers as the measure, thus rejecting expansion to cover activities undertaken as being 'in connection with' or 'in relation to' those granted. This, it is hoped, will guard against broadening the spending authority to embrace everything that affects them peripherally as in the United States under the commerce clause.

Claims to compensation for foregone tax sources which were relied on when creating government debts or government establishments have a strong appeal. Transitional in nature, they seem to be so limited both in duration and in use as not to pose serious or continuing problems about the use of surplus federal funds. Yet they have done so. They were absent in the Swiss and German federations which restructured existing unions of members having no sizeable individual outstanding commitments. They have chiefly been resorted to when previously independent units enter into association, notably in Australia and Canada.

In both, the confederates had been self-governing colonies for some little time. They had had their several budgets. Construction and development projects had taken them into the capital market. They were in debt in different amounts. On the other hand, each had buildings and public works for which proceeds of borrowing had been used. Such of these assets as found their use in connection with responsibilities to be assigned the dominion (commonwealth) were to be – and were[9] – made over to the federal government. Too, import duties had been by all odds the major tax source of nearly all the colonies and they were losing it. Negotiation of the details of settlement, taking into account these factors, absorbed much of the attention of the constitution framers. The process at times resembled more a business merger than the devising of a new political association.

8 The Australian constitution alone gives clear recognition to such use in its provision that 'the revenue of the Commonwealth shall in the first instance be applied to the expenditure of the Commonwealth' (s 82). The US constitution deals with it inferentially by stating that '[t]he Congress shall have Power to lay and collect taxes to pay the Debts ... of the United States' (art 1, s 8, cl 1).

9 BNA Act, Schedule III; Commonwealth of Australia Constitution Act, s 85

In neither country was the effect of the assumption transient. In Canada, the primary provision directing dominion liability for the provincial debts[10] was given artificial content by ascribing as the basis of bargain and agreement a fixed dollar limit to the debts of each original province.[11] It did not precisely conform to the real amounts although it reflected them. Any whose debt was more than the stated amount should remain liable for it and for paying interest at five per cent on the difference to the dominion;[12] as to the Maritime provinces only, if it was less the dominion would pay them interest at that rate on the shortfall.[13] The then current liquid assets of the province were to become the property of the dominion but credited to the province against the real balance of the debt assumed.[14] Thus a formula of compromise and concession produced a scheme having artificial elements and envisaging a standing series of interest transfers in one direction or the other.

This was complicated enough in itself. The addition of new provinces to the dominion made it more so. Some were recited as having no existing public debt.[15] They were accorded payments equal to interest at five per cent on arbitrary amounts representing hypothetical permissible debt levels. British Columbia was accorded debt recognition by reference not to its own situation but to bringing it into line with existing provinces,[16] Prince Edward Island by an anticipated maximum incurrable debt in lieu of the arbitrary limits assigned the original provinces.[17] After the addition of the prairie provinces, an imperial statute discarded outright the debt assumption premise for subsidies[18] save for the crediting of interest deductions.[19] The prenatal provincial debt had been initially the real focus of this subsidy even though in its quantification that reality was tempered by political considerations. It became a pure fiction, providing provinces a basis for incessant jockeying for supplementary grants to compensate for having assertedly been disadvantaged by the original debt assumptions and by the ongoing series of artificial adjustments.[20] Once

---

10 S 111
11 S 112; cf s 142 (division of Province of Canada debt between Ontario and Quebec), s 114 (Nova Scotia), s 115 (New Brunswick).
12 S 112
13 S 116
14 S 107
15 Manitoba Act, 1870, 33 Vict., c 3, s 24 (Can.): Alberta Act, 1905, 4–5 Edw. VII, c 3, s 19 (Can.); Saskatchewan Act, 1905, 4–5 Edw. VII, c 42, s 19 (Can.)
16 Order in Council Admitting British Columbia into the Union, May 16, 1871, schedule, s 2
17 Order in Council Admitting P.E.I. into the Union, June 26, 1873, schedule, para 3
18 BNA Act 1907, 7 Edw. VII, c 11, s 1(6) (U.K.).
19 Hence Newfoundland entered on a special basis unrelated to its debt, actual or constructive: BNA Act, 1949, 12–13 Geo. VI, c 22, s 24 (U.K.).
20 See *Report of the Royal Commission on Dominion-Provincial Relations* (Rowell-Sirois Commission), Book I, at 41–45, Book II, at 126–7.

the historical content was scrapped, its usefulness for confining federal discretion ended and the debt assumption operation went the way of the Cheshire Cat.

There is no indication that Australia gave serious consideration to the Canadian model of a fixed level of colony debts assumed. They were not overlooked; but the framers elected to make permissive and discretionary what if anything should be done about them, by providing that 'Parliament may take over from the States their public debts or a proportion thereof existing at the establishment of the Commonwealth' with arrangements specified respecting the interest on any that might take over.[21] With parliament thus having a free hand, the states had no occasion to use the relative position of others as the pretext for a claim of right, as in Canada. Moreover the more general terms of other sections authorizing[22] or directing[23] parliament to establish state participation in federal revenues with no principle of division set out as a guide blunted any importance state debts might have had. Redundant, the provision about them remained unused. Through needless apprehension of prospective termination of section 96's broader authorization, the limitation to debts existing at the establishment of the commonwealth was stricken out in 1910 by constitutional amendment. This erased even the rhetorical relevance of those debts. It cleared the way for negotiating federal aid for the current deficits states were regularly incurring. By a further constitutional amendment in 1927,[24] the groundwork was laid for the Loans Council which now dominates central-member financial arrangements in Australia. With it historical debt assumption as a critical factor in federal subventions lost even its spectral relevance.

A new Canadian constitutional arrangement need not reckon with the existing provincial debts. So the foregoing recital is not immediately relevant. It does show though that selection of an existing balance sheet as a basis for federal transfers is illusory.

The tax sources, notably import duties, lost to the newly created government, had been relied on not only to meet debt payments but also to sustain the machinery of government in the associating units. A replacement was required. That was at any rate true in Canada and Australia. Constitution makers sought alternative provision for defraying the costs of government, together with the satisfaction of outstanding indebtedness. In each, they handled them on the same general lines.

Canada started out by setting a compromise-born base-line figure payable to each original province 'for the Support of their Governments and

21 Commonwealth of Australia Constitution Act, s 105
22 S 96
23 S 87
24 S 105A

Legislatures' plus 'an annual Grant in aid' of eighty cents per capita using the 1861 census, with Nova Scotia and New Brunswick benefitting up to a ceiling from increases shown by later censuses.[25] Until 1907 each additional province was dealt with like Nova Scotia and New Brunswick but with a hypothetical (and ordinarily greatly inflated) postulated initial population used for the per capita computation unrelated to any census.[26] Individual further concessions were made: New Brunswick had been allowed by way of exception to continue her existing lumber dues[27] and was to receive 'an additional allowance'[28] of a set amount for ten years; British Columbia was to get annual payments in consideration of the conveyance of a railway belt to the dominion;[29] Prince Edward Island,[30] Alberta,[31] and Saskatchewan[32] claimed and were allowed additional amounts because none of them had public lands to be sold or leased – the first a base amount, the latter two on a per capita basis. Alberta[33] and Saskatchewan[34] also, by reason of their having no public lands, were awarded flat sums for a limited time 'to provide for the construction of the necessary public buildings.'

Except for built-in per capita escalation of the New Brunswick and Nova Scotia 'grants in aid,' the 1867 act appears to have assumed that its arrangements would stand firm.[35] That expectation proved false. Almost from the beginning, provinces clamored for 'better terms' and the federal government responded in a series of ad hoc restatements of particular amounts. The original substitutionary premise of the program, with implied constraints on federal disbursement, was dissipated if the figures were vulnerable to constantly renewed political dickering. The Manitoba Act tried to avert this by a daclaration, futile as Canute's decree, that the sum shall be in full settlement of all future demands on Canada.'[36] By 1907, the need for a fresh start led to replacement of the basic figures set by earlier legislation. Updated ones graduated by population were sub-

25 BNA Act, s 118
26 Manitoba Act, supra note 15, s 25; B.C. Order in Council, supra note 16, schedule, s 3; P.E.I. Order in Council, supra note 17, schedule, para 6; Alberta Act, supra note 15, s 181; Saskatchewan Act, supra note 15, s 18.
27 BNA Act, s 124
28 S 119
29 B.C. Order in Council, supra note 16, s 11
30 P.E.I. Order in Council, supra note 17, para 5
31 Alberta Act, supra note 15, s 20(1)
32 Saskatchewan Act, supra note 15, s 20(1)
33 Alberta Act, supra note 15, s 20(2)
34 Saskatchewan Act, supra note 15, s 20(2)
35 This assumption is confirmed by the circumstance that the additional award to new Brunswick by s 119 was expressly for a ten-year term, while the global arrangement under s 118 was without limitation as to time.
36 Manitoba Act, supra note 15, s 25

stituted for the 'grants' payable a province for 'local purposes and the support of its Government and Legislature.'[37] Nonetheless the transfers formally designated as 'provincial subsidies' survive virtually unchanged.[38]

They remain as thresholds, a relic of historical arrangements. With a useful minor role in providing discretionary funds for provincial use, they have been swamped in importance by other programs. Many of these have specific objectives. They are often shaped by recurrent political bargaining in dominion-provincial conferences. That approach to transfer payments is more appropriately explored later.[39] Here one need only note that the initial technique of tying subventions to real or constructed data to compensate the provinces for lost or non-existent revenue sources supporting their public services proved as ephemeral as the analogous concept of debt assumption.

Australia too followed a consistent pattern as to both. The realization missing in Canada that any settlement was necessarily ambulatory led to mention of a transitional term in each of the relevant constitutional provisions. Because of the loss of the colonial customs duties, the states were, under a clause denigrated as the Bradden Blot, to be entitled to three-fourths of the net proceeds of federal customs receipts '[d]uring a period of 10 years after the establishment of the Commonwealth and thereafter until the Parliament otherwise provides.[40] In that period, by another section, 'the Parliament may grant financial assistance to any State on such terms and conditions as the Parliament thinks fit.[41] And, '[a]fter 5 years from the imposition of uniform duties of customs, the Parliament may provide, on such basis as it deems fair, for the monthly payment to the several States of all the surplus revenue of the Commonwealth.'[42] Under this scheme, federal customs replacing the colonial ones were relevant both as constituting the basis for a fractional participation, temporary but extensible, to assure the states a source of replacement income and to start the time running after which amounts however derived excess to federal needs could be turned over to them at parliament's unfettered discretion. That discretion was the eventual and ultimate determinant. The customs duties surrendered, like the debts assumed, were a starting

37 BNA Act 1907, 7 Edw. VII, C 11 (U.K.)
38 The provisions of the Provincial Subsidies Act, R.S.C. 1970, C P-26, are a simple continuation of those in acts of the same name in each of the preceding Revised Statutes starting with 1886, picking up the additions consequent on the accession of new provinces.
39 Infra, at 87–9
40 Commonwealth of Australia Constitution Act, s 87
41 S 96
42 S 94

datum leaving parliament an authority open-ended but expected at least to continue and most likely to augment the transfers to the states. That did not happen. Parliament terminated the three-fourths sharing immediately the mandatory ten-year period expired. It eluded the implicit directive to allot income in excess of federal needs to the states, by establishing a trust account to fund future federal programs and diverting to it receipts beyond current budget appropriations, on the theory, which was judicially approved, that no surplus revenue then remained. Of the three related sections, only section 96 allowing the grant of financial assistance on such terms and conditions as parliament might see fit remained operational. The states were tacitly invited to seek federal subsidies but parliament had a completely free hand in awarding them. The constitutional amendment of 1927 and the Loans Council established pursuant to it have institutionalized state dependence on federal financing in the manner to be explained hereafter. It suffices here to note that present arrangements in no way resemble what the framers had in mind.

Whether employed, as in Canada, as formulary data or alluded to, as in Australia, as motivating guides, the relationship between the members' altered position in consequence of federation and the quantum of subsidies is an extinct consideration. That was foreseeable. The situation at the point in time when a constitution is adopted will change both as respects the means at the federal government's disposal and the uses to which it and the members wish to put them. For the framing of a new Canadian constitution, neither debt assumption nor abandonment of an existing field of taxation seems a real issue. Still, examining the record of futile recourse to them is not just an academic exercise. It illustrates how static norms for federal grants give way to political claims resolution with its capacity for continuous reorientation, where the federal holder of the purse strings is dominant.

The recognition of national crises or of member disparities as appropriate grounds for diversion of federal funds to the members invokes future contingencies not set scales.

No constitutional text specifies national crisis as authorizing transfers. Yet it is clear from the historical record that it does.

In the United States the issue has been discussed only tangentially. In sustaining the Social Security Act in *Steward Machine Co* v *Davis*,[43] Cardozo J writing for the court remarked:

During the years 1929 to 1936 when the country was passing through a cyclical depression, the number of the unemployed mounted to unprecedented heights ... The problem had become national in area and dimensions. There was need of

43 (1937) 301 U.S. 548, at 586–7

help from the nation if the people were not to starve. It is too late today for the argument to be made that in a crisis so extreme the use of the moneys of the nation to relieve the unemployed and their dependents is a use for any purpose narrower than the promotion of the general welfare.

He thus brought the act within the prevailing analysis of article I, section 8, clause 1. McReynolds J's observation in dissent that the legislation being permanent in character was not defended 'upon the basis of emergency'[44] concentrates on the holding and neglects the opinion. While for strict stare decisis only the first counts, for purposes of prediction the second is often more significant. The expansive interpretation the United States has given federal powers in general and the spending power in particular has obviated reliance on crisis as enlarging congressional power; but it seems reasonably clear that grants attributable to it will not be challengeable.

Canada and Australia reacted identically to the situation created by world war II by a structure of grants to each province or state to make up for a federal take-over of productive tax fields, notably the income tax. Both countries, foreseeing that the war would increase federal expenses enormously and federal taxes correspondingly, wanted to spread the burden evenly across the country. This, it was felt, would not be done were incomes diversely eroded by reason of large differences amongst provincial or state income taxes. To achieve uniformity, all must be subject to the same tax, of necessity federal. Without their income tax proceeds, however, all would be in financial difficulty, some more, some less depending on the degree of use of that tax. To substitute for those proceeds, the federal government would make grants. Reflecting in principle the same considerations as historically had operated as regards the loss of customs duties, an important distinction was that here the arrangement related to what was seen as an interim suspension of member taxes for however long the common government might be coping with a common crisis. Despite similar ends and means, the procedure for establishing the program differed between the two countries. In both, the amount of the grants was negotiated in view of each member's special circumstances but the negotiation was in Canada a preliminary to, in Australia an outgrowth of, the blanketing federal legislation.

The Rowell-Sirois Commission, to help solve the problems of the depression of the 1930s, had proposed that such an arrangement be put on the agenda of a dominion-provincial conference.[45] With the coming of war, the commission's recommendations were shelved but provincial va-

44 Ibid, at 609
45 See *Report*, supra note 20, Book III, s B, ch III, v

cation of the income tax field surfaced as an item for a projected dominion-provincial conference. That fell through; but, echoing the earlier initiatives, separate bargains were struck with each province for its disuse of taxing authority in consideration of a federal allotment. The requisite provincial and federal legislation to carry them out followed.

In contrast with the Canadian origin in projects of bilateral settlement, Australia started with an existing model of federal control. The ingenious avoidance of a 'surplus' through diversion to a trust account[46] left the commonwealth grant assistance to the states 'on such terms and conditions as the Parliament thinks fit.'[47] It had thought fit to make per capita grants 'subject to the terms of any agreement made between the Commonwealth and all the States, and adopted by the Parliament.'[48] Parliament's role in conditioning the terms on which grants were made was thus established practice. In 1942, four companion federal acts were adopted.[49] These, without formally forbidding state income taxes, imposed a very heavy federal tax and provided that from its proceeds an amount calculated by reference to what the states' equivalent taxes had been producing should be set aside for payment to them. Any state which persisted in taxing income would be excluded from sharing. There had indeed been discussions with the state looking toward a mutually agreeable revenue-sharing program but, these having come to nothing, parliament prescribed the program unilaterally.

Switzerland provides another illustration of crisis-occasioned revenue sharing. The categorical distribution of tax competence there reserves direct taxation generally for the cantons. With the coming of world war II, federal expenses particularly for the defence establishment grew astronomically and the confederation, first by emergency decrees and then pursuant to constitutional amendment, levied a tax first styled *impôt de crise* and later *impôt pour la défence nationale*,[50] of which thirty per cent was set aside for and turned over to the cantons.

Except for the US example, these were grants by the federal government to the members only in form. In substance, they were the converse, with the members desisting in favour of the federal government from resort to normal revenue sources subject to a reserved claim of stated magnitude on the proceeds of the federal tax as a replacement. When first

46 See Menzies, *Central Power in the Australian Commonwealth* (1967), at 95.
47 Commonwealth of Australia Constitution Act, s 96
48 State Grants Act, Commonwealth Acts, No 4 of 1927, s 6
49 States Grants (Income Tax Reimbursement) Act, Commonwealth Acts, No 20 of 1942; Income Tax (War-time Arrangements) Act, Commonwealth Acts, No 21 of 1942; Income Tax Assessment Act, Commonwealth Acts, No 22 of 1942; Income Tax Act, Commonwealth Acts, No 23 of 1942.
50 See Aubert, supra, chapter 2, note 3, at 59.

introduced, all were framed as temporary measures. None eventually expired with the occasioning crisis. By the device of tax rental agreements in Canada, by statutory extension without limitation of time in Australia, and by a series of legislative and constitutional postponements of the terminal date in Switzerland, what they had adjusted to in time of emergency was continued as regular practice.

The consensual element was formally present at the inception of only the Canadian program. But general concurrence in the initial propriety of the arrangements may be seen in the adoption of constitutional amendments in Switzerland, by the fact in Australia that the, unsuccessful, court challenge to the 1942 legislation[51] addressed itself to the single issue of the propriety of parliament's unilateral prescription of state tax abeyance as a condition.

One might well be wary of accepting 'emergency' with the indefinite contours of the ambiguous US reference as justifying transfers. Everywhere else resort to it has appeared in the context of one kind of emergency – war – and with an express time limitation to the needs incident to that emergency. Limited thus, it does not threaten federalism. A visible peril to the country's life so transcends normal constitutional relations that all the members would be expected to join with the central government in agreeing on countering measures. Certainly no constitutional challenge to them will or should succeed.

Experience shows, however, that, starting in emergency, they do not end with it despite express provision that they will. Though crisis be a proper basis for federal rationing of member revenues, resort to it can stretch to establish permanent general member dependence on federal funding, unless there be safeguards in two respects, one as to what circumstances amount to a triggering crisis, the other for resolving when the crisis and its derived grant authority ends. Neither was present in any of the cases examined. War was ordinarily the relevant and it is perhaps the clearest kind of crisis. Other perils to the country's existence might conceivably operate similarly. A great defect of each was the exercised freedom to dishonour the condition of temporary operation.

The proposed draft allows for the contingency of crisis while providing the necessary restraints. It confines federal spending ordinarily to paying for the operations of the federal government in executing powers constitutionally assigned it.

This restriction is doubly qualified however. The Canadian Equalization Council can allow some leeway: but only for establishing a reserve, not for enlarging the range of current disbursements even in a crisis.

51 *South Australia v The Commonwealth* (1942) 65 C.L.R. 373

What does that is the exception, allowing the use of federal money freed of the basic limitation 'with the unanimous concurrence of the Provinces.' If and while there is a situation of sufficient gravity to induce provincial consensus, the boundaries on federal spending will be fixed not by the constitutional list of federal functions but by the range of extension to which there is provincial agreement. Any one province by withholding or withdrawing its assent can contain federal spending authority within its regular limits. Neither by outright prescription nor by the tactic of herding the provinces in line through fear of getting left out can the federal government retain control. If, as I am confident, the provinces' appreciation of the common interest is enough that they will concur whenever there is a genuine threat to the country and yet their diversity of interests and policy is such that unanimity will not outlive the peril, the proposal combines provision for the necessary flexibility with an efficient check on its misuse.

Debt assumption, interim substitution for lost tax sources, and crisis, however valid as grounds for authorizing the use of federal money for non-federal purposes, all are special and transitory considerations. In principle they should cease to operate with the retirement of the initial debt, member development of alternative tax resources, or the passing of the crisis. In practice, all decay first into mere facades for and finally into ancestral ghosts of federal spending programs. The one basis with continuing vitality, involving no perversion of the constitutional design, is the employment of federal funds to smooth out disparities between the provinces.

Acceptance of a degree of community responsibility for improving the lot of less affluent members is not peculiar to federations. Even as loosely knit an association as the United Nations has done what it could to institutionalize it. At the other end of the spectrum, unitary states have established special schemes designed to bring depressed regions up to a national standard. Within federations, state or provincial programs channeling resources preferentially to their needier localities abound. It would be most surprising were the social empathy so pervasively manifested lacking as between units who have chosen by federating to proclaim a special relationship with each other.

In some it is the stated basis for a mandated distribution amongst the members.[52] Others by failing to name it among the matters to be taken into account seem to deny it any significance.[53] Others again which assign tax fields by category rely chiefly on fixed ratios of federal and member

---

52 Constitution of Argentina, art 67(8); Constitution of the Socialist Federal Republic of
    Yugoslavia, art 258; Constitution of India, art 275(1)
53 Constitution of the Republic of Venezuela, art 229; Constitution of Brazil, art 25.

entitlement neutral as to need while maintaining it as a relevant factor for the discretionary disposition of the proceeds of some particularly important federal tax.[54] Still others are wholly mute about it.[55] The United States and Australia are in the latter group. So except by indirection is Canada. Yet in all three it has been operationally even though not constitutionally recognized.

Its role in the United States has been peripheral. Starting late because of the shaky constitutional grounding, federal grants out of tax-derived funds were from the outset primarily grants in aid not of the states but of programs which the federal government was interested in promoting but was under then-current constitutional conceptions unable to regulate. That has remained their main thrust. Despite the virtual disappearance of any limitations on its regulatory competence, congress for various reasons desires state involvement as administrative auxiliaries in the implementation of its programs. Earlier formulas of shares equal for each or tied to population or tax revenue generated meant, particularly when accompanied by matching-grant conditions, that the poorer states, already strapped to discharge their proper functions, had the same obligations imposed on them as on others if they took part in a program but without provision of any special allowance to assist them. Some recent legislation has modified earlier practice by including relative indigence as one among the elements in figuring the amount of the grant. It is not the only one. Nor has it stopped the major portion of federal grant money from flowing to the wealthier states under prevailing formulas. A handful of funds has, it is true, been established for improving the lot of designated distressed areas[56] by analogy to predecessor appropriations for disaster relief,[57] but with them the standard pattern is one of direct federal administration. The states are not used to any great extent as intermediaries, although doubtless some financial strain is taken off those in which such projects operate. The teaching of the us experience seems to be that relative member deprivation neither manifested as a concern at the time of confederation nor textually alluded to in the constitution, while it will not be dismissed as irrelevant, will not weigh heavily as a consideration.

The Australian framers gave the matter more thought but still not enough. They provided distinctly, even elaborately, for federal transfers to the states. Preoccupied with customs duties which had been the finan-

54 Federal Constitution of the Swiss Confederation, art 41 ter (national defence tax); Basic Law of the Federal Republic of Germany, art 107
55 Federal Constitution of Austria; Constitution of Mexico
56 Eg, Appalachia
57 They are only analogous and not parallel, since disaster relief is an intrinsically temporary response to some natural catastrophe, by contrast with longer term measures for dealing with systemic regional disparities.

cial mainstay of most of the colonies, they assumed that those would provide comfortably for the anticipated modest expenses of operating the commonwealth establishment and leave a substantial margin to take care of those of the states generally. They thought they were in the main giving due consideration to each state's needs by measuring by collections within the state borders,[58] its share in the ten year guaranteed three-fourths of federal customs and excise[59] since as colonies most of them had been living on those tax sources, and by the expectation that within ten years a federal surplus would arise which parliament would turn over to the states (but with no basis of distribution prescribed).[60] Nevertheless they were fully conscious of respects in which state situations differed currently and vaguely foresaw other contingent differences. For the former they provided by authorizing the assumption of existing state debts and more particularly by a special concession to Western Australia for temporarily continuing import duties.[61] For the contingencies they empowered parliament at its discretion to 'grant financial assistance to any States,'[62] thus implying that some might need assistance. With the end of the ten-year guarantee and the intervening sleight-of-hand elimination of any surplus, the surviving effective clause was the imprecise one authorizing the grant of financial assistance. The basic policy adopted by parliament was a general per capita grant to all the states. But simultaneously Western Australia claimed and was allowed a supplemental amount because of its relative lack of independent means. So later did others of the less industrialized states. The Commonwealth Grants Commission Act[63] in 1933 substituted for ad hoc applications of the policy a systematic structure to carry it out. It functioned until 1973. 'The principle ... that the States which operate under basic financial difficulties should be extended a helping hand in order that the standard of service available to all citizens, regardless of whether they live in one state or another, should not be far out of line' was officially characterized as 'long-established.'[64] There was not only direct resort to that principle, which was intended to be and was exceptional; it also influenced the scale of the non-uniform per capita payment award by the Grants Commission to every state as the chief

58 Commonwealth of Australia Constitution Act, s 89. S 89(ii) specified certain deductions but the distribution principle was as stated.
59 S 87
60 S 94
61 S 95
62 S 96
63 Commonwealth Acts, No 3 of 1933
64 See the statement of the Acting Prime Minister to the June 1959 Premiers' Conference, quoted in Else-Mitchell, supra, chapter 2, note 46, at 264.

element in state grants. The initial muted recognition of relative state disadvantage as justifying transfer payments was fleshed out to become a body of working practices where it explained some awards altogether and played a part in the computation of the great bulk of them.

The BNA Act to some extent in its provisions for debt assumption but more particularly in sections 118 and 110 bears evident marks of the bargains struck amongst the provinces in order that all might be able to bear the costs of local government. The alternatives were seen as either allowing the provinces to impose indirect taxes or providing federal subsidies in varying amounts. As between them, the fathers of confederation elected for the latter.[65] They thus tacitly admitted a differential capacity without outright declaration and structured a subsidy schedule which they hoped would permanently compensate for it.[66] That hope proved illusory. Almost at once provinces started claiming additional amounts becaues of their lack of effective access to resources of a kind available elsewhere. That was taken into account too in the settlements made on new provinces as they entered. Each new special arrangement created further complications as to comparative position. It is widely recognized that, be it because of geography, weather cycles, federal transportation, credit and trade policies, or world supply and demand conditions, there have been and are unevenly distributed ups and downs in economic potential. Save for the economic purists for whom efficiency of resource allocation is a fetish, there is full agreement that giving a hand to provinces with means substantially below the general level is a proper use of federal money. In the Provincial Subsidies Act[67] that consideration survives only as an explanatory anachronism and in program-linked subventions it is put aside.[68] But a formula incorporated in the Federal-Provincial Fiscal Arrangements Act[69] constitutes a mechanism for accomplishing it. It systematizes the operation of a working principle which started almost with confederation itself, at first only fuzzily. Application to only one of several streams of federal transfers to the provinces does not diminish the significance of that principle's acceptance, especially since it is the main stream for money flows unpolluted by programatic elements. For the sake of completeness, mention must also be made of the various

---

65 See *Parliamentary Debates on the subject of the Confederation of the British North American Provinces*, 3d session, 8th Provincial Parliament of Canada (1865), at 93.
66 BNA Act, s 118 directed that the grants therein provided 'shall be in full settlement of all demands on Canada.'
67 Supra note 38
68 See Dyck, The Canada Assistance Plan: the ultimate in cooperative federalism, (1976) 19 *Can. Pub. Admin.* 587.
69 R.S.C. 1970, c F-6, s 8

measures for the relief of particular distressed areas[70] but, like their US equivalents, these are direct federal undertakings. With them the question is not what federal payments to the provinces are proper but whether spending, like beauty, is 'its own excuse for being.'

That is the central and ultimate question.

This chapter so far in examining spending grounded on special considerations has been non-committal about it. It has concentrated on their status as justifications of and controls on state or provincial subventions.

As justifications, debt assumption, revenue source absorption, and crisis differ from member disparity. They are situation-oriented; it focuses on a relationship. They are to meet costs involved in establishing or preserving the common authority; its concern is with member claims grounded on formation of a partnership to be put in a position approaching their fellows. Both seem reasonable justifications. There is a difference of scope. The situation-oriented group being reimbursing, the grants corrective of inequalities redistributive, each justifies only outlays serving its respective purpose. Neither is a blanket authorization for federal spending.

Using federal money for the support of federal organs and functions directly established by the constitution seems self-evidently proper. But on what principle may a federal government raise or apply funds for matters within the range of provincial competence? It might be argued that control over crown assets was historically an element in the sovereign's prerogative freely exercisable except as displaced by legislation; but, in a federal system, each level of government acts as or for the sovereign only for its part of the totality of authority. It might, on the other hand, be argued by analogy to the private law of companies that contributions extraneous to institutional purposes are ultra vires; but private law and public law are distinct universes. More fundamentally it might be said that so-called federal property is, like all public property, really the people's property; its holding by government is as their agent; then, absent a statement of express authority,[71] the scope of implied authority is crucial.

The obvious alternatives are authority to use it in the execution of such of the principal's affairs as have been delegated to the agent or to dispose of it in any way regarded as beneficial to the principal (that is, the people). The latter alternative would indicate a status as general managing agent to

70 Eg, those authorized by the Department of Regional Economic Expansion Act, R.S.C. 1970, C R-4
71 The situation may be different in Australia, where s 96 of the constitution, which permits parliament to 'grant financial assistance to any state on such terms and conditions as the parliament thinks fit,' may be read as express authority.

whom others are subordinate. It fits ill the theoretical conception of federalism. But it has prevailed in practice.

The proposition sometimes advanced that federal spending is permissible for the achievement of national purposes is objectionable only as lending itself to that broad reading. Given a steady adherence to recognizing as properly national purposes only the specific areas as to which power is delegated to the federal government by the constitution, it would just express vaguely the endorsement of expenditure for its own operations. That leaves it a large range of activity – enough probably to realize through the proposed grants of authority as to transportation facilities and commodity transactions most of the items for instance, of the historic Macdonald National Policy. In general, it encompasses establishing a structural setting to support provincial initiatives. But, if 'national purposes' be taken as extending to selection of the pattern of local priorities within the potential thus created, the proposition invites federal specification of a uniform life-style[72] not necessarily congenial to the different communities in Canada. It is open to criticism not because it is false but because it is equivocal. Recasting it as suggested to authorize federal spending 'in effectuation of the powers granted to or recognized in the federal government' removes that vice while leaving a federal capability to create an institutional environment hospitable to effective provincial dynamics. That is enough. To go further and prescribe the pace and direction of implementing programs would jeopardize the diversity of local policies respect for which distinguishes federal from unitary states.

Spending can like taxation be made a disguise for regulation. In a federation, with each level having its own fields of competence, it can be and often has been an unguarded gate for the central government to enter on the provincial domain. The recipient of a transfer payment will usually be a province or one of its local governments. It need not be; payments can instead be directly to individuals or enterprises on terms of their conforming their conduct to federal policy on matters over which the federal government has no direct command.

Whether other governments participate or not, an unqualified turning over of funds to others falls within the definition of spending and so within the federal power. That never actually happens with spending which bypasses them. It does sometimes as to transfers to provinces. When it does, the transfer is perforce without any regulatory taint.

The archetypical situation is that exemplified by section 118 of the BNA

---

72 This seems to be what some of the judges in *Victoria* v *The Commonwealth* (1975) 134 C.L.R. 338 would bring about.

Act and section 87 of the Australian constitution of entitlements being given the provinces and states according to a fixed formula with no strings attached. Discretion as to the use was to be wholly theirs and in no way federal. Even now section 118 and the corresponding provisions which accompanied the addition of other provinces, as embalmed in the Provincial Subsidies Act,[73] are free of regulatory vice and of being objected to on that score as improper exercises of the spending power.

At the other extreme are programs which yoke together grants to members and requirements, often very detailed, which must be satisfied in order to qualify for sharing.

Particularly in the United States, given the unconfined sprawl of the commerce clause, and in Canada and Australia to a minor extent, the annexed conditions deal with matters coming within federal classes of subjects. Then there is no need to rely on spending power. What is present is simply an Olympian instance of a make-or-buy decision. If administrative or politic considerations lead to enlisting the agencies and services of another willing government rather than using one's own for effectuating a program which might be undertaken directly, all that is involved is a choice of techniques. There is the question, not a very serious one, of borrowing by mutual assent the administrative apparatus created by another for doing a job. But whether the agencies or services be in effect hired or supplied gratuitously, spending is not the issue. While every coupling of program prescription and payments is regulatory, federal transfers to the provinces as executants of otherwise valid parliamentary legislation (or for that matter provincial transfers to the federal government or to each other as executants of a province's legislation) are on no different footing than expenditures in support of the government's own establishment and direct operations. There is no question of parliament's doing indirectly what it could not do directly where the spending is for something it could do directly but chooses not to.

A federal decision to distribute funds among members necessarily calls for prescribing what each is to get. Entitlement may or may not be made conditional on adoption of programs in line with federal policy on matters left to them by the constitution.

If it is, it is just as unrealistic to label the legislation an appropriation as to call similarly conditioned measures taxation. A fairly common practice of earmarking the proceeds of a particular tax for allocation to the members for use in furthering federally specified objectives has contributed to confusion by making available both spurious categorizations for measures essentially regulatory. Whether because of constitutional

73 Supra note 38

doubts or because the internal and external pressures for federal activity were weak at first, the tying of grants started late and modestly with the designation of the general use to which they were to be put. From there to establishing controls against their being misapplied and from there in turn to ever more elaborate specification of terms governing permitted use were natural stages. The variety and dimensions of meticulously defined grants, all recognized as immune from challenge as exercises of the spending power, came to shrink the effective discretion of the states and provinces over large areas. The consequent erosion of functional competence was aggravated by calling for matching grants. Thereby programs of federal inspiration occasioned drains on the members' own revenues. Indeed they not infrequently provided the bulk of the funding. At times they were left irreversibly committed after withdrawal of federal participation. There seems to be a growing inclination to recede from categorical grants to the milder constraint of block grants. Even they hobble the recipients' policy choices. The less fully they are told how the money shall be used, the more room there is for each to determine the relative strength of the claims competing for development in line with local needs and sentiments. Yet every sharing system in which use is indicated is a temptation to shift priorities.

A critical question is the terms on which transfers are to be allocated. Considered by themselves, unpolluted by conditions, they can be accepted as a fully justified exercise of the spending power, indeed an important instrument for realizing the benefits of federation. Those benefits consist of not simply allowing but aiding each member to achieve self-realization. In contrast with the homogenized polity characteristic of a unitary state, federalism supposes that the individuality of the members will be preserved and strengthened. To that end common funds may be employed.

Various schemes of distribution uncontaminated by conditions have been tried, some with more or less mechanical criteria, others dependent on the exercise of discretion.

Instances of the former type using a historical basis, such as the assumption of outstanding debts or an estimate of surrendered revenues, of some surrogate for them, or of an amount to support provincial government, have already been noted. Such frozen figures make for a policy-neutral division. If adhered to, they would be supportable as at least having had at one time a rational basis. Since in practice they thaw because of inevitable progressive irrelevance, recipients cannot be indifferent to federal reaction to their programs. The incessant reopening they invited proved a political nuisance. They are now out of fashion, existing only as historical relics. Revival of that technique is neither to be expected nor to be recommended.

The simplest scheme would be to give the same amount to each member. Aside from simplicity, there is little to be said for it. It has therefore almost never been employed. Universal participation has been accepted as a policy but with shares related to some designated variable among the members. One, perhaps the crudest, is population. Another, usually associated with the revenue derived from a particular mode of taxation, is the proportionate amount of that tax which is collected within the state or province. In contrast with these single-factor criteria, complicated combinations of factors have been devised to accommodate an array of political pressures.

These arrangements all have the merit of exorcising from the distribution its potential for use as a way of exercising federal control of matters beyond federal competence. That risk exists only when a discretion as to the conditions or amount of entitlement is retained. Yet the virtue of federal transfers to the members is precisely the existence of a capacity for discretionary apportionment. If the shares were simply to go back to the locality of origin, routing through federal channels would be just a collection service. Any administrative benefits involved – obtainable without constitutional objection in any event by agreement – would be somewhat offset by the constraint to co-ordinate the tax pattern and by whatever extra costs might be incurred. More significant, apart from those incidents, the treatment would reproduce what would happen were there no federation.

Some at least of the prosperity of the more prosperous members seems fairly attributable to the very fact of federation. The benefits, a spinoff from the commercial, transportation, and like policies of the central authority, accrue unevenly, fluctuating with economic and technological change. Those members that are relatively disadvantaged at any given time have a just claim to partake of the increment created by association. Direct payments to them are a mechanism for satisfying that claim. Moreover, federation by its very existence manifests a feeling of there being a closer link with fellow members than with the outside world. Thus empathy joins with political morality as a foundation for sharing.

From family assets each of the family may ask that the necessaries of life be provided. Thence flow the considerations which should guide the exercise of discretion. The difficulty arises in working them out. There questions of two different orders arise. First, there is the question of choice as to what kinds of difference between states or provinces should be taken into account to determine an equitable allocation in conformity with the fair shares principle. Second, by whom should that choice and the parcelling out of available funds in line with it be made? To the first, the remainder of this chapter addresses itself. The second is dealt with in the next chapter.

The basic principle itself has been put clumsily as that of equalization and grotesquely in the proposition that payments should be made so that no province is below the average. Besides the constant jiggling which that would entail, the corollary would be that no province could be above the average, a moving point reflecting the relative position of all and ultimately bringing all to a common level.

Reduction of gross disparities, however, is a realistic goal. Its attainment may invoke exercise of discretion at a single stage or at two successive stages. One always involved is selection of the criterion for entitlement.

If the chosen criterion is essentially statistical, the exercise of discretion is exhausted with its choice. Allusion has been made to distributions geared to population or to tax collections. These leave only computational accuracy to be resolved. They have, however, no appreciable correlation with the member disparities sought to be smoothed. Tax collections as a yardstick may even aggravate them. Population signals not relative lack of economic but possession of political resources. A more pertinent objective indicator which has attracted some attention is per capita income. Its calculation, while less precise than population and tax collection data, is nevertheless possible within a reasonable range. It does obviously though doubtless not exactly vary with the degree of provincial participation in the synergistic wealth-creating consequences of association. It has therefore a decent claim to attention. That it should be used alone and always as the governing consideration does not follow.

Alternatives to those data-controlled criteria involve an element of subjective judgment and thus of discretion not only in their selection but thereafter in their application.

One is need. It epitomizes succinctly the adverse situation for which federal spending is an appropriate corrective. But need is essentially relative. For present purposes, the gap to be filled is not simply that between the existing and the desired inventory of resources. Every community like every individual wants more than it has means to buy. Need here refers to the greater size, in comparison with other provinces, of the gap between the package of services generally accepted as proper and the capacity to supply them. The make-up of the package of deprivation calls for an exercise of judgment. So, with plural provinces qualifying, does the decision how best to deploy the always finite federal funds in partial redress of their several needs. Use of need as a criterion is therefore only a threshold exercise of discretion which entails further exercises.

It focusses on demand, the optimizing of the satisfaction of claims to consumer enjoyment of the benefits of political association. The converse principle which emphasizes supply differentiates on the basis of relative member resources. Reference to per capita income represents a crude approximation to it. But its flow-of-funds approach neglects non-market elements going to enhance or detract from the quality of community life. It requires the same sort of second-order judgment following the decision to use it as the criterion as does need.

A third standard is relative tax effort. Our culture premises that a claim to assistance in the relief of unsatisfied needs deserves consideration only in behalf of claimants who make a serious effort to cope with them within the limits of their independently possessed resources. For political entities, tax potential is the main one, supplemented mildly by goods and services provided for a price. A state or province that neglects to enter on the tax fields its fellows harvest and to glean with ordinary diligence may risk having its failure reckoned against it. Like heaven, the community stands ready to help those who help themselves.

Each of these three has been resorted to as a basis for apportioning available funds. All of them involve value judgments, need and tax effort quite obviously, relative resources collaterally. Each manifests concern with a particular deviation from a national mean, the condition I have propounded as a valid objective of a federal grant program. For each, details of quantifications must be resolved but within a fairly narrow range once the relevant criterion has been selected.

In practice, the tendency has been to use them, in combination with each other and also with the different type exemplified by population.

They are sometimes corrupted by splicing with them federal qualifications about the use of funds, as where grants for highways refer to topography or for education to school-age population as bearing on need or, more generally, in the recent experimentation with block grants, notably in the United States. Such measures which, even though gently, impose federal priorities on the objectives of provincial expenditure warp provincial choice. They cannot be regarded as having strictly the character of correcting provincial disparities. That belongs only to distributions which leave expenditure fully discretionary with the members' own policy-making organs.

Need, resources, and tax effort are all program neutral, each open to comparison on a common scale constructed from accepted measurable elements, and each indicative of position on the provincial totem pole. Any of them is therefore prima facie suitable as a basis for federal grants. The difficulty is that advance commitment to or regular dependence upon any of them risks offsetting adjustment of member fiscal or development policies. Preserving the neutrality of fund transfer as an equilibrating mechanism precludes freezing a formula so that it can be made a basis for prediction, for the same reason that an external input to the policy mix on its own merits would blunt it. There must be continuing discretion to assign participation so as to reflect not merely an appreciation of the ingredients and dimensions of a fixed criterion but a selection and balancing of criteria. The consequential elimination from consideration of a potentially distorting factor outweighs the curtailment of planning.

Yet, like any discretion, it presupposes for its proper functioning an exercise by agents competent and concerned to achieve the ends it is designed to serve. To that matter I turn now.

PROPOSED PROVISIONS

A There shall be a Canadian Equalization Fund administered by the Canadian Equalization Council.

B The fund shall consist of the net proceeds of duties on import and of such federal revenues whether derived from taxation or otherwise as are in excess of expenditures in execution of federal purposes under section ( ) and of any reserve provision thereof which the council may from time to time direct.

C There shall be a Canadian Equalization Council of one member designated by each province and one federal member. Each member shall have such qualifications and be chosen in such manner and for such term as the jurisdiction designating the member shall by law provide. Compensation payable from the Canadian Equalization Fund shall be the same as that of a justice of the Federal Supreme Court.

D The council is an independent constitutional organ which and each member of which shall not act under or for any particular government.

E The council shall at least annually requisition for and the federal treasury transfer pursuant to requisition to the fund funds which are excess within the terms of subsection (B). The net proceeds of duties on imports shall be transferred to the Fund at the end of each federal fiscal year.

F The council shall at least annually allocate the fund among the provinces to the end that the resources of each may be such that it can provide government services at a level worthy of Canadian life and shall cause to be paid to the general revenue funds of the provinces without condition their respective allocations, provided that it may establish a contingency reserve for disasters.

G The cost of operation of the council including such staff as it may constitute shall be paid from the fund whose accounts shall be federally audited.

With one offbeat exception discussed below, every system for distribution employed to date has been unsatisfactory. Accepting that even under the best conceivable arrangements the reach will exceed the grasp, the continuing festering general discontent everywhere with what has been tried and the resultant flow of measures tinkering with the allotment of shares reveal the existence of a pervasive radical flaw. Without its identification and then its elimination, there can be no tolerable resolution of provincial-state claims to participation in federal revenue. To that end the creation of a novel mechanism is proposed. Its novelty makes its unfamiliar details seem complicated, more so than they actually are. However, it does call for exposing what that radical flaw is and explaining the workings of the device designed to eliminate it.

I start from the premise expounded in the preceding chapter, that the legitimate objectives of federal grants – and the only ones to be authorized under a new constitution – are three: the effectuation of delegated federal functions, the coping with crises, and the smoothing of variations amongst provinces with regard to the resources available for pursuing their several public goals. The frequent injection of programatic elements has been a major factor inducing the use of inappropriate modes for distribution. Those, as requiring policy choices, belong to and should be dealt with by the political organs of government at that level of a federation charged with deciding policy about the matter at hand. The ease with which control of the purse can be a vehicle for control of policy has diverted attention from that critically important consideration. Unlike the ultimately subjective values which shape substantive policy, fairly applicable external criteria exist for each of the three legitimate objectives of federal spending – the equitable claim to a partnership share in the benefits from the national enterprise as well as the scope of federal functions and the existence of crises. Differences amongst them as to those criteria imply corresponding differences in the mechanics of implementation. But for none of them do the central political organs have special qualifications to decide. In casually assuming that role, at the outset as a matter of course and thereafter as incidental to substantive policy prescription, they strayed into a course of growing complexity and constant frustration. There has been an increasing readiness to define the factors on which decision is based and to seek an outside input of views but the final word is still regularly reserved to federal political authorities.

A common evolutionary pattern is discernible.

The initial naive response is to leave the matter to unguided direct bargaining between legislators or constitution framers.

The United States first confronted it in connection with the distribution of surplus funds arising from the sale of western lands. Jockeying in congress produced a grant program masquerading as a loan which accommodated diverse member sentiments as to the basis of awards.

Elsewhere it is found at the very birth of the constitution in the compromises worked out for settling the terms of union. Indirectly by the assignment of tax fields, directly by including provision for grants, constitution framers often struck an original global bargain reflecting imperfectly if at all a sensitiveness to the justifications for diversion of federal funds to the constituent units. That happened in both Canada and Australia.

In Canada the fathers of confederation, looking at what they had created and finding it good, optimistically pronounced it 'in full settlement of all demands upon Canada.[1] It was not to be. Almost immediately modifications were demanded. With this lesson before them, the Australians more realistically accepted that their initial arrangements were temporary and provided an ongoing mechanism for revision after a lapse of time. In both, the reordering of the grant structure was treated as a matter for parliament, hence for the federal government of the day, to decide. The provinces or states proposed; the federal godhead disposed.

Canada started out treating it as a matter of unabashed political dickering. Australia early on inaugurated a system of funneling state applications through a State Grants Commission whose recommendations served as a basis for parliamentary appropriations. Eventually Canada too turned to a similar technique for processing provincial claims. Still, this simply regularized the preliminary screening, leaving the outcome to legislative decision. With state and province requests never quite fully met, the parliaments in both countries sought to deflect discontent by further formalizing structures emphasizing consultation with the applicants. The pattern differed. In Australia a federally appointed Grants Commission considered state submissions as a basis of its recommendations, regularly followed, to parliament for legislative awards. In Canada, a continuing committee of ministers of finance and provincial treasurers was created as an adjunct to an intricate network of recurring intergovernmental conferences, dominion-provincial and ministerial. Both were ways of introducing a mass of external economic data and of enlisting staff expertise in the process of a decision which, however, remained finally that of the federal political authorities – in Australia because of control over composition of the Grants Commission, in Canada because the committee members, ordinarily deputy ministers, could 'bind their principals only to the extent the principals permit,' leaving it to 'the politicians [to] make policy decisions ultimately rather than the experts.'[2]

In both the grant aspect was submerged in a larger universe of member-centre financial relations. In Australia, because of the curious development of the reserve to avoid surplus funds discussed above, provi-

1 BNA Act, s 118
2 Kear, Cooperative federalism: A study of the Federal-Provincial Continuing Committee on Fiscal and Economic Matters, (1963), 6 *Can. Pub. Admin.* 43, at 53, 54.

sion of an infrastructure which dominated state expenditures was the concern of a distinct body, the Loans Council. In Canada, following the tax rental agreements, assignment of tax fields and allocation of grants had become so entwined that the latter was dealt with not separately but as part of a total package. Moreover, in both, the continuing presence of flat-sum statutory entitlements for each state and province and even more an accompanying levy of conditional special-purpose grants shrunk appreciably the volume of funds falling to be dealt with to the end of correcting disparities. A signal feature of each scheme was that at the end of the day only a distribution in line with dominion (commonwealth) government policy would be adopted. While the special arrangements were useful for informing that policy (and incidentally on details of administration), the choice among weight of the criteria for comparative evaluation was by political authorities at the federal level. To say that they were highhanded would be unfair. Not to recognize that they had the upper hand would be naive.

These arrangements were scrapped in both Australia and Canada. Each substituted as the primary determinant in revenue-sharing a statutory formula cranking in designated statistical items to be employed by the minister to calculate entitlement. Australia has reserved to him power to make discretionary increases. Canada has not. As in the early days of confederation, parliament tinkers with the standing plan by adjusting amendments. Stated amounts are still frozen in the legislation and the miscellany of special purpose conditional grants continues, thus leaving adjustment grants as only a segment of the transfer tableau.

The current situation reflects a desire to minimize the recurrent need for exercise of discretionary decision by political authorities. Hence it resurrects the aspiration of the pioneer Canadian legislation to establish a fixed scale but modified from an arithmetic constant to an algebraic equation whose members though specified are stated as variables.

The Australian reservation and the Canadian series of amendments suggest that as before the attempt will fail because new conditions require and will always require new response. Change is the one thing permanent. The record forecasts the frustration of measures which hobble a grant program from marching with the times.[3] That has happened with fixed scales of payment. A hardened list of the governing factors and their weighting, though probably somewhat more resilient, has also a built-in obsolescence for which the same fate is to be expected.

The Swiss and the German evolution has been similar, complicated by

3 See, eg, Federal-Provincial Fiscal Arrangements and Established Programs Financing Act, Stats Can. 1976–77, c 10.

the detailed constitutional assignment of tax fields to one or the other level.

In Switzerland, a series of designations of taxes as for federal collection has been characterized by dividing the yield between government levels in varying proportions, the cantonal share amongst the cantons on bases – population, tax origination, etc – differing from tax to tax.[4] There is also the familiar array of conditional subsidies for matters which the federal goverment sees as of national concern. These types between them comprised the major part of the confederation's contribution to the cantons yet a large imbalance amongst them persisted. It may even have been aggravated because of the very items chosen to regulate sharing of the reserved cantonal fraction of designated taxes to smooth the remaining unevenness. Successive ad hoc responses by the federal council, most often connected with tax legislation, were relied on until 1949. In that year, an *arrêté* of the council instituted a system which consisted in classifying the cantons as 'strong,' 'average,' and 'weak,' using a complex formula specifying the mix of factors to be taken into account. The Swiss, like the Australians, recognized and dealt with prospective revision, not however as in Australia by a vague open-ended reservation but by setting a two-year term to the classification with the federal council passing on it anew at biennial intervals. The consequence is a periodic referral to federal political determination. The tendency to shy off from piecemeal alteration of intricate mechanisms except to correct clearly revealed defects imparts a measure of stability so that Switzerland has been able to live with this mildly ambulatory scheme without radical changes.

In the Federal Republic of Germany too percentage participation in the take from particular taxes is common.[5] Since the taxes affected are by all odds the greatest revenue producers, this is the principal source of federal subventions. The participation ratios as between the two levels are subject to biennial revision accomplished by federal legislation. But the composition of the council of states, the second chamber of the parliament, with ministers from the länder as members, tends to insure that the decision, while a political one, will not just give ear but will give heed too to the wishes of the länder. This settles their aggregate share while leaving what each of them receives dependent on constitutionally prescribed factors – population and local tax source.[6]

4 See Aubert, supra, chapter 2, note 3, at 283–93.
5 Basic Law of the Federal Republic of Germany, art 106(3)
6 Of the two main taxes, the income tax division is based on the amount of local tax collections, the value added tax division on population, but only as to 75% of the proceeds of that tax, the other 25% being assigned to the disadvantaged länder to help them attain the minimum percentage and so to reduce the volume of interstate transfers required.

The budgets of the less wealthy länder, though largely fed by the shared taxes, can still be on a starvation diet. Most additional nourishment is furnished in a way unique to Germany, of transfers between states rather than to them from the federal government. Its operation involves features not found elsewhere – the establishment of a länder tax rate uniform throughout the nation, the negotiation by the council of states, with its state ministerial and senior civil service composition, of the amounts due to or from each land, and construction of the adjusted tax capacity of each land as the criterion of entitlement and obligation. That construction, tempered by some allowance for special considerations recognized as relevant, rests basically on taking into account a land's revenue from its own (including municipal) taxes and its portion of the shared taxes. It is then compared with their average tax capacity per capita which is a multiplicand and with land population as multiplier. A minimum percentage relationship between each land's adjusted tax capacity and the average tax capacity is set by federal law (hovering slightly above ninety per cent). Shortfalls of the sum of land tax receipts below what that percentage of average adjusted tax capacity multiplied by population would produce are made up to it by transfers from länder whose receipts are above it. Need as such is rejected in favour of an artificial and thereby more objective standard of relative tax capacity. With the taxes from sources reserved to it plus the land's fraction in the shared taxes thus supplemented by interstate transfers, gross disparities are substantially smoothed. That reduces the occasions for direct federal transfers on an individual basis. It does not entirely eliminate them. There still are some. Normally they are for 'joint tasks,' collaborative activities specified by an agency with representatives from both levels, rather like conditional grants with the significant difference that they are not unilaterally selected by the federal government. A very modest additional unconditional direct transfer of federal funds is exceptionally made to relieve a distressed state.

This drastically simplified account reveals a highly ingenious scheme for minimizing the dominance of federal political authorities while enabling continuous adjustment in aid of the less fortunately circumstanced states. It avoids the Scylla of delusive rigidity and the Charybdis of federal political hegemony. Its complex structure presupposes a combination of elements – among them uniform state tax rates, a state-oriented federal upper house, and an interstate bargaining procedure – not found and perhaps not feasible elsewhere. It deserves consideration as an alternative, should the method proposed in this chapter be found unattractive or prove ineffective. Incorporating the special elements on which it rests would, however, involve sweeping changes throughout the Canadian constitutional milieu. I hesitate to recommend it as a model only because while it, amongst all those examined, is the one successful approach, its success seems to depend so much on its special setting.

The United States affords no helpful guidance. The early compromise formula base for distributing the surplus from public land sales was so short-lived (because that surplus vanished) that it could not be appraised as a long range measure. When federal subventions reappeared, they were all program-oriented and thus conditional. Usually maxima and/or minima for state entitlement were included. Those might and often did include references to whatever special difficulties of particular states their representatives could induce congressional colleagues to accept as relevant. That allowed some consequential differentiation from the diverse base-line formulas that were prescribed. But concern with states' disparity was always only incidental to the primary use of subventions to induce state conformity with the adoption of substantive policies on matters dubiously susceptible to direct federal control. That was the unvarying pattern for over a century. In 1972 a timid and reluctant move away from categorical grants was made.[7] It applies to only a minor part of the total grant program. It is not truly general in that, while there are minimal restrictions on what the states can use the money for, twice as much goes to the municipalities which can spend it only for specified purposes whose breadth and variety gives wide latitude but not complete freedom. An initiative of a president with a politically hostile congress, it was enacted grudgingly, on a trial basis for a limited term. The century of categorical grants has produced a psychological climate and, still more, a web of institutional structures from whose centralizing drift there may be no escape. The present arrangement is surely a transient phase. But the course of future development is wholly uncertain.

Canada's travel down that same road has not gone as far, yet far enough that there are like obstacles to an about-turn to be reckoned with. Supposing them to be still surmountable, a new departure cannot much longer be delayed. It ought not be along paths that experience has shown to be blind alleys.

The eventual collapse of all schemes to relate the distribution to set amounts or fixed formulas could have been foreseen. Life, for a political community as for any organism, implies change. Static arrangements, however well suited to the original situation, cannot adapt sensitively to economic and social shifts which are bound to come. To keep arrangements in line with current conditions there must be some agency charged

7 State and Local Fiscal Assistance Act of 1972, Pub. L. 92–512, 86 Stat. 919

with ongoing response. To do so that agency must be empowered to exercise judgment and should have the qualifications for exercising a sound judgment. The sole constraint should be a specification of the desired objective, with wide discretion as to the means of attaining it. The critical questions calling for consideration are first the structuring of an agency to exercise the discretion, then its operations.

The proposed Canadian Equalization Council has no direct ancestor.

All the unvaryingly failed plans have left the ultimate decision to political authorities. Other than the very special setting in West Germany, that has meant to federal authorities. True, the proliferation of ingenious structures has evidenced a real impulse towards informing the process by views from outside the federal or even outside the political establishment. But all have left it with the last word.

Commonly the constitutional texts simply leave the allocation of grants among members to federal legislatures. Commonly these have undertaken at the outset a direct exercise of the discretion, responsive to what political weight claimants could exert on the government federally in power rather than on their objective relative situations.[8]

Given the always finite pool at its disposal, politically motivated awards of largesse, like patronage employment in government posts, irritate unsuccessful while seldom fully satisfying successful applicants. Seen as on balance support-enlisting mechanisms too dubiously effective to compensate for the frictional nuisance occasioned by the tugs and pulls incident to dealing with the constant recurring need for renegotiation, there has been a steady drift away from the primitive procedure. Its net inconvenience has spawned mechanisms, embodied in custom, legislation, or latter day constitutional proposals or in a combination of them, designed to convert it from an exercise in power jockeying to an ostensibly objective assessment.

The forms have varied. Further detail than that given above seems in order.

In Canada, a Continuing Committee on Fiscal and Economic Affairs with senior civil service representation from each province and from the federal government was created aş the secretariat of the recurring federal-provincial conferences. Its primary mission was to elaborate agreed proposals and presentations from which would emerge fiscal

8 The situation is analogous when at the time of elaboration of a constitutional text which makes particularized assignments of shares in or partitions tax sources, the support sought instead of being for a government in power federally is for agreement to enter into confederation, but it too is an instance of the strength of political resources rather than the weakness of economic ones being the dominant consideration.

programs, with consequential effects on provincial sharing of the federal revenues,[9] statutorily tied to the results of applying the fiscal programs. Although the committee's proposals might be expected to and usually did shape the determinations, they were for the federal-provincial conferences, conclaves of political authorities, to make and to bring to fruition by conforming legislation. The terms of the agreement as thus implemented effectively governed the amount of supplemental payments to provinces from the federal share. They were effectively tied to it by a standard formula.

In Australian finance, because of the need to make up for the country's initial shortage of physical plant, borrowings figured largely. Hence the resources to be allocated there come more from loans than from taxes. An integrated program for approving capital outlays and the loans to enable them has been a dominant feature in the commonwealth's financial arrangements. A Loans Council composed of ministers, normally premiers, met upon call to do this, somewhat in the way Canadian federal-provincial conferences pass on division of taxes, but without matters having been filtered through a group like the Canadian continuing committee. Instead, a federal official, the coordinator-general, was instituted as a continuous liaison with state officials in preparing details to serve as the agenda for Loans Council meetings. With this less formalized initial screening, the Loans Council was less regularly provided with data for decision than are the Canadian federal-provincial conferences and its decisions were more open to political arm-twisting. Withal the have-not states remained hard put to provide standard government services of average quality. Another body, the Commonwealth Grants Commission, was created concerned with federal subventions to provide relief. Its membership of three, all federally appointed with no statutory qualifications prescribed, made recommendations following a conventional hearing which when adopted by parliament as they always were set the amounts of states' participation in the federal bounty.

Elsewhere other forms of organization have been devised to plug outsiders into the allocation process. In India, the constitution calls for a Finance Commission, all members to be appointed like the Australian Commonwealth Grants Commission by the federal chief executive, parliament being authorized to legislate qualifications and manner of selection.[10] However the greater part of the subventions fell in practice outside the commission's own competence; it had to consult about them with the

9 Except of course for the constitutionally frozen payments specified for the provinces, discussed supra, at 61–3
10 Constitution of India, art 280

federal Planning Commission and federal ministries, which led it to recommend its own transformation. In Malaysia, the constitution specified a National Finance Council composed, much like the Australian Loans Council, of the premier, an additional federal appointee, and one member appointed by each state governor;[11] however its functions combined those of Australia's Loans Council and Grants Commission with particular emphasis on projects at each level involving capital outlays. Brazil's Tribunal of Accounts was a particularly detailed effort to assure an impartial and qualified agency; while the president was to appoint, his selections needed approval by the federal senate, were to be 'from among Brazilians over thirty-five years of age, morally fit, having recognized legal, economic or financial knowledge or knowledge of public administration,' and were to enjoy salary, tenure and similar guarantees parallel to those of the Federal Court of Appeal.[12]

Simple or complex, these have a common feature. In all, the additional mechanism serves only as a consultative or recommending organ. Ultimate decision still rests in the federal political authorities – parliament and, with it controlled by the federal executive, the government of the day. Typically, too, by leaving appointment to the latter or, even where there are representatives named by states or provinces, the group chairmanship, they preserve a fundamentally centralizing thrust over the framing as well as the fate of members' claims to shares. Without imputing to them either insincerity or highhandedness and fully recognizing that they make some contribution to an exploration of relevant considerations, they do not get at the root of the problem – a conclusion confirmed by the scrapping of such special instrumentalities in Canada and Australia and by their attrition elsewhere.

The deserving poor are not always the politically powerful. Indeed there may well be an inverse relationship. If membership in the former category is the true basis for federal subventions, to leave them dependent on those who are sensitive to the latter is to risk distortion of judgment. What the draft accomplishes is a more appropriate location of effective decision.

Two grounds of opposition to it, one lofty, one grubby may be expected.

Democratic theory generally and our own political tradition specifically accepts as axiomatic that the power of the purse rest with the legislature. Any proposal at odds with that principle should be suspect. This one is not.

11 Federal Constitution of Malaysia, art 108
12 Constitution of Brazil, art 72, para 3

The relatively late origin of the principle as a political postulate – in England in the mid-seventeenth century after John Hampden's resistance to the ship money, echoed in the United States as a claim at the time of the American Revolution and then anchored in the constitution, in Canada with the realization by the 1840 Act of Union[13] of the primacy of the elected assembly in money matters – is sufficiently close in time and clear in outline to let one see the substance behind the cliché. In each instance a demand that taxing and spending decisions be for popularly elected representatives to make triumphed over a regime of independent non-responsible control. Though the situation in each case happened to be one where the body which directed the raising of public money would be the same as that which authorized its spending, that was not what was at issue. The circumstances did not present and the principle therefore did and does not deal with the need for union of those functions. What was sought was that neither should be left to the discretion of persons not chosen by the affected public.

Anything satisfying that condition respects the postulate. The draft proposal does. The federal legislature which has a free hand in the raising of revenue, the state or provincial legislatures which have a free hand as to its expenditure, are alike popularly chosen by the constituencies which will be affected by those respective exercises. So invocation of the power of the purse as a theoretical objection is misconceived.

Anyway it probably only supplies an elegant rationalization for a more earthy ground which really explains the regular retention of definitive decision by the central political authorities. They are unwilling to let go of what is cherished as a support mechanism for themselves. Even outright grants uncontaminated by conditions can generate political advantage. The hope of getting them is good political bait. Their award can be exploited to advantage at election time. The potential as a political resource virtually guarantees official opposition to any suggestion of a neutral allocative body.

Preliminary screening by federally appointed agencies or departmental staff may at most temper, it never erases that. Their recommendations will be biased in the same direction – in their case not with a view to vote-getting but out of the normal impulse characteristic of institutions to empire building. Self-interest is the great although probably often unacknowledged obstacle to receptiveness to any alternative to present practice.

In other contexts, the political branches have slowly progressed toward relinquishment to non-political organs of comparable support-enlisting activities.

13 3–4 Vict., c 35 (U.K.)

It has been a long time since Saint Louis sat under the oak tree, much less long since Coke admonished James I that causes were to be decided not by his majesty's 'most excellent right reason' but by 'the artificial reason of the law,' and still more recently that bills of attainder fell into desuetude in Britain and were forbidden expressly by the United States constitution. Only yesterday did the Senate of Canada cease to concern itself with divorces. While a dwindling area of private legislation perpetuates it, it is now widely accepted that competing claims of legal right should be left to courts, whose members possess appropriate professional qualifications and whose independence is safeguarded.

There has been a similar development in connection with public employment over the last century. Before then it was accepted and expected that it might without impropriety be used to attract and reward political supporters. A relatively few positions are still reserved for recruitment on that basis but by and large public service commissions now direct a hiring process free of partisanship.

In both cases, the evolution was marked by and may have depended on the existence of a corps of persons seen as qualified both by their command of a relevant discipline and by their independence, to whom decision could be entrusted. Surviving areas where those conditions are doubtfully satisfied remain more largely open to manipulation for political advantage. A conspicuous one is government contracts. A call for an alternative arrangement can thus fairly be asked not only to point out the unsatisfactory character of that which has existed but to incorporate features which give a fair prospect of meeting the prerequisites of informed and independent action by the replacing agency.

This, it is submitted, the Canadian Equalization Council does.

What it envisages is in substance a Supreme Court of Welfare Economics. Displacement of the appointment power from the federal executive to the provinces is a marked departure from the traditional practice regarding supreme courts. It is deliberate.

Experience shows that federally appointed courts have drifted always to acquiescence in centralized control. I do not mean to suggest either deliberate subversion to that end by the appointing authority or subservience by the judges to the central government's wishes after appointment. The candidate field from which names will be brought forward when vacancies occur primarily consists of those whose associations and consequent sympathies have been nationally oriented. It underrepresents those with a regional focus. Whatever provincial laws may provide respecting appointments, one can anticipate that they will not narrow consideration in the way that central appointment in practice has done.

That characteristic feature of the candidate pool is aggravated by the circumstance that, once appointed, removal from the local milieu and day-to-day exposure to that of the national capital scene in time blurs the vision of outlying claims and interests. The courts, which must continuously process a stream of cases brought to them, cannot readily escape that. The council has not the same need to be almost uninterruptedly in session. It can schedule meetings so as to let members keep closer personal contact with conditions and sentiment in all sections of the country. In calling for certain decisions 'at least annually,' the draft does imply that meetings shall be held every year. How many there shall be within the year and for how long is left to the council's discretion. It would seem that more than one will be needed, also that the time required to dispose of the agenda at each will be inversely related to their frequency. These matters had best be left flexible, dependent on circumstances. Mention of audit of the costs of operation of the council including provision for a staff appointed by its suggests that it will have available a secretariat, preferably modest in size, for record filing and analysis and general clerical functions. The secretariat would probably have a permanent location which however need not and perhaps ought not be in the national capital – but there would be no need for council members to stay there or indeed to go there except at times. Proper discharge of their important responsibilities while probably a full time job may most appropriately be performed by garnering and harmonizing grass roots observations. Their modus operandi like their qualifications would be those of social scientists.

Expected working practices of that kind serve to maintain the values furthered by provincial designation – a broader spectrum of viewpoints conducive to a more balanced assessment of relevant subvention criteria and of their application to the current position of claimant provinces. Both encourage wide representation of the diversity found within the outer limits of a common professional background. For the 'imperfect competition' model of decision-making with the federal government as the 'dominant firm,' which has up to now prevailed, is substituted a process in which a variety of premises have more chance of being represented and of effectively competing. There may be no test for whether the results will be better but certainly they will be better balanced.

And balance in judgment is imperative for the decisions about allocation to have the quality of acknowledged fairness to each member of the federal family essential to avoid chronic discontent.

To the possible objections that rather than establishing a balance, the proposal creates a reverse imbalance replacing federal by provincial dominance, what with all but one of the council's members provincially designated, there are two answers. One is somewhat formal, the other substantive.

The formal answer is that the council will have for decision competing claims of the provinces inter se and not between the federal and the provincial levels. The council will be dealing with an Equalization Fund as to all of which all federal entitlement is gone. Any federal interest in the fund so sterilized will be at a low level. With virtually nothing to gain, that government will be very weakly motivated to take sides in a competition between the provinces. The existence of any common front amongst them against the federal government predicates a conflict of interests shared by them counter to some federal interest. That is not present under the plan proposed. Espousing no particular position, the federal authority cannot properly be said to have been subordinated. Only with questions which will occasionally arise as to what 'expenditures' are 'in execution of federal purposes' so as to diminish the Equalization Fund could it be otherwise. Those will, however, as involving constitutional interpretation, be settled in the manner and by the tribunals performing that function; there relative federal-provincial influence on the scale of subventions is irrelevant.

This formal answer to the change of overdexpanded provincial authority is ingenious but a bit disingenuous. A firmer ground inheres in the two clauses relating to its structure and status.

Provincial appointees clearly preponderate numerically. Were they a monolith, that might be important. The major accomplishment of the proposal is to muffle the control of any one participant in the decision. Leaving half or more or indeed any multiple places to be filled by the federal (or any one) appointing authority would encourage a team spirit leading to the formation of a voting bloc whose cohesion could distort the process of group decision. What is wanted is, as with a court of law, the composite judgment of qualified individuals, each governed solely by his reasoned assessment of the relevant materials, with situational bias by reason of internal structure eliminated as far as possible. Differentiation between nominees or nominators would affront the perfect parity of position the pattern of professional appraisal presupposes. There is no more reason to expect that others would line up against the federal appointee than that they would against the appointee of, say, British Columbia or Newfoundland or Quebec and thus none to support a claim to special recognition.

The characterization of the council as 'an independent constitutional organ' and the directive to members not to 'act under or for any particular government' affirms the judicial analogy.

It may well be that at the outset some appointment authorities will give little heed to the exhortation. That should correct itself. Increasing experience with the council will almost certainly demonstrate that an appointee's personal calibre determines his weight in its deliberations.

There will be just too many possible combinations to make the stance of the advocate or the horse trader persuasive to a majority of the group over the long run. Their colleagues will come to discount them as special pleaders whose interjections are even likely to be on the whole counter-productive. Seeing their ineffectiveness for getting material payoffs, appointing authorities will settle for the plaudits accruing from naming persons who on their merits command the esteem and can attract the support of their colleagues. Therefore, disregard of the principle of independence, and there will at first be some, will be a temporary phenomenon.

The clause is, however, more than a mere statement of general principle to guide the attitude of those appointing and those appointed. It entails at least two substantive consequences.

The status of 'independent constitutional organ' gives an assurance of tenure. The provinces and parliament can indeed provide by law for their appointees' terms and thus, by virtue of the inalienable power of successive legislatures, make new arrangements. They cannot terminate retrospectively the position of incumbents. Once appointed, they hold office under the constitution, not under the appointing government. As such, they are shielded from removal on account of changes of government or of discontent with what they or the council have done with regard to current allocations. The provision for compensation contained in the preceding clause is a further assurance of independence, both in removing payment from the budget of particular governments and in assimilating it to an external stable standard, the compensation of federal Supreme Court justices.

Not acting 'under or for' any particular government, the council stands outside the federal as well as any provincial family of agencies. It is a direct constitutional creation whose authority derives from and whose procedures are subject to direction and control by neither. Subject to any limits imposed by the constitution as construed by the tribunal competent to rule on constitutional issues involving inter-level relations, it is fully autonomous.

A significant consequence is that what it does cannot be made the subject of questions in the legislature, either provincially or federally. Nor can an appointing jurisdiction presume to instruct its appointee either as a condition to or during the term of his appointment. In these respects again, it is like the judiciary. It is not answerable to any government nor is any government answerable for it. The provinces can urge their claims before it just as they can before courts but to treat its determinations as a matter of government policy or administration would be censurable as a grave parliamentary impropriety.

Eleven members (possibly one or at most two more by reason of the creation of additional provinces) constitute a small enough group to allow genuine collegial deliberation yet big enough to give reasonable assurance of a representation of different viewpoints. The idea is as with a court to benefit by the composite judgment of qualified and impartial individuals. It need not, nor ought it to be arrived at using the methods and materials of courts. Those of the social sciences would seem more appropriate and would probably be resorted to by the council. To it the matter should be left. But, mechanics aside, the quality of involvement in a decision ought to be analogous to that of an appellate court. There will be dissents. There may not always be full conformity to any or many members' notions of an optimal result. What is essential is the presentation of serious alternatives and their personal assessment by members. By happy coincidence there are enough appointing authorities in Canada that a range of positions would be canvassed yet few enough for the members themselves to hammer out a decision instead of leaving the real thinking to staffs or committees. The fortuitous fit in numbers between the historic political units and a body well adapted to doing the job, rather than any abstract considerations, dictates the manner and extent of dispersal of the appointing authority.

The quality of potential appointees is still more important than their quantity. The draft deals with it indirectly but, I believe, effectively.

In leaving the qualifications and the manner and term of designation to each appointing authority, it conforms to the constitution's distaste for centralization and detailed prescription. Here, as in other respects, belief that home-grown measures will be locally more acceptable and not demonstrably less wise than remote control is manifested.

But it is required that these matters be provided 'by law.' They cannot be tacitly left to whomever is entrusted with the appointment (presumably the constitutional executive) to be dealt with without restraint. Nor can he even receive by delegation authority to set them. Those are matters as to which the law must not just provide but must itself make provision. One consequence is to gain for the plans chosen the benefits hypothesized from the publicity attending legislative proposals. Another, more certain and more important, is increased stability. Although legislatures will be free to change the law when and as they see fit, they will, as was noted, not be able to do so as to an incumbent, vested once he is appointed with a constitutionally supra-provincial (or supra-federal) status. Remodelling the statute to establish prospectively a preferred pattern is not impeded but neither disgruntlement with him nor a wish to open a place for the party faithful can fuel changes, with current effect, in the law. Independence in decision-making is protected without prejudicing flexibility or local autonomy.

Independence for an assembly of dolts or party hacks would be no boon. The plan proposed has merit only insofar as it tends not simply to the retention of incumbents but to the selection of competents. It does. The two interact.

The council members will depend on their personal qualities for whatever authority they exert with their fellows. While party affiliation and regional orientation may very likely be factors affecting the initial choices, and coalitions be based on them, that will, because of the council's size, if for no other reason, be a transitory phenomenon. The recurring shifts in party control characteristic of Canadian provinces tell against the long survival of party alignment. No regional grouping unites a majority of the eleven members; any combination requires external support. Failing these two extraneous stimulants to voting solidarity, each member's impact will depend on his personal qualities and the respect they inspire in his colleagues. His effectiveness as a team member will be seen to turn on that. Protected in his independence and depolarized as a guiding principle, he will be sensitive to that fact. So will the appointing jurisdiction. It will not be indifferent to its appointee's reputation, knowing that he cannot be called on to serve as its representative. Acquiescing in that, even if reluctantly, it will still be credited or scorned for the kind of appointments it makes. Its action will be conditioned accordingly. The whole setup is calculated to produce ultimately a practice of true merit appointments.

Note that the draft does not specify anything about residence or domicile. If a province wishes to legislate such a qualification, it of course may. Equally it may omit it. Canadians are used to having members of parliament elected elsewhere than their province of residence unlike the situation of the United States where it is a condition of eligibility.[14] It rests for the province to decide. Certainly well-qualified candidates are distributed across the country. Certainly too it is desirable that members, although not representatives of any particular jurisdiction, be familiar with local conditions and sentiments so that there may be brought forward in council deliberations the full mix of elements which blend to constitute life in Canada. That familiarity will most often but need not always be associated with local residence. With the post-appointment links as tenuous as they would be and the sole significant increment to the appointing authority recognition as making good appointments, the council should eventually turn out to be composed of a group whose members were recognized as knowledgeable in the relevant discipline, the economics of welfare.

14 US constitution, art 1, s 2, cl 2; s 3, cl 3. The Australian constitution, s 34, requires only that a member of the House of Representatives be 'a subject of the Queen,' without imposing any further residence or domicile requirements.

A body of that kind should have the choice of criteria for allocation of grants left to it. The general tendency has been to specify particulars – need, population, revenue origin, relative tax effort – for use simply or on some weighted formula as a basis for apportionment. A case may be made on political or economic grounds for each of them in a given context.

Nevertheless none of them and no one set of them is always or everywhere satisfactory. Each has side effects the neglect of which may seriously distort its operation. The economic and social setting of resource bases, fiscal legislation, and life styles in which they operate change continually, with concomitant changes in the appropriateness of the fixed basis for distribution. There is corresponding ongoing refinement of relevant professional understanding and doctrine. Useful for channeling the discretion of a lay group, the itemization of considerations controlling decision is a dysfunctional clog on the application of specialist competence. The end to be achieved may properly be set out, and it is in the draft proposal. The means for achieving it had best be left, as it is, to the judgment of the council, weighing the prevailing situation in the balance of its collective expertise.

The end is unambiguously stated. It is to apply the fund at its disposal toward making available to each province 'resources ... such that it can provide government services at a level worthy of Canadian life.' Admittedly that is inexplicit. It seems, however, to embody the nucleus of general agreement on sharing.

From the very beginning, the existence of depressed areas in Canada has been acknowledged as has the legitimacy of their claim to partake of the consequential benefits of confederation which they are not circumstanced to capture. A structure that forces them to make repeated applications to the federal government creates the false impression that they come seeking handouts rather than restoration in some measure of the value which their membership as components in a common market, framed by federal tariff, transportation and contracting policies, indirectly contributes to the aggregate but which escapes their direct grasp. For them it is demeaning. For the other provinces, it is corrosive of the mutual respect each member should have for each other's identity and status.

In using standards of nationwide life as the reference and in entrusting its systematic determination on an objective basis to an impartial expert body, the situation is put in its true perspective. This is as far as one can go by way of an affirmative directive.

The expression, 'equalization,' is eschewed except as a convenient shorthand designation for the fund and the council. The sentiment occasionally voiced that all should be made equal is manifestly absurd. Even were such an evaluation possible it would require almost daily jiggling to maintain that condition. Encompassing a levelling down as well as a levelling up, it would discourage initiative by withdrawing its rewards and rewarding its neglect. It goes beyond anything that either the needy provinces claim or the prosperous ones would accept. What is practical is sought in a grant system leading not to but toward equality.

The one flat limitation on the council's discretion is that provincial allocations shall be made 'to the general revenues of the provinces without condition.' Each province, I maintain, is the best or at least the legitimate judge of its own priorities. The practice of conditional grants might not be quite so grossly inimical to provincial authority if the conditions were set by a body like the Equalization Council rather than by the federal government. Yet it too would tie provinces to policy preferences other than their own. What a province does with funds furnished it is primarily its own business. The possibility that they would be flagrantly squandered can be heavily discounted by virtue of the recipient government's accountability at the polls. Because the use made of them would normally fill some of the gap between the province's services and those 'at a level worthy of Canadian life,' there should be some motion toward smoothing out existing disparities. Successive evaluations by the council, it may be expected, would take into account whether the record of the grantee provinces showed them addressing themselves to that broad end. More specific than that it should not get. The ranking of health, highways, housing, education, industrial development, law enforcement, environmental protection, family assistance as objects of improvement is for the provinces. The council will concern itself only with the composite provision of governmental services, not with the components. Even that will be only one piece of evidence in the complex process of evaluation.

Welfare economics, it is true, is not and may never become a discipline rigorous enough to generate scientifically precise decisions. Its doctrines are still evolving, even erupting. Wide differences of opinion amongst its members exist. But the same is true to my personal knowledge of law and, it seems, of personnel administration. Yet, as was noted, the core of agreement in those fields has been found great enough to permit of entrusting decision to those specially versed in them. Welfare economics has matured to a comparable position of sophistication and shared ideas. Evidence of this is its literature, for the lay reader as arid and abstruse as theirs.

A qualified deciding authority, the definition of a goal, and freedom for that authority to choose measures looking to its attainment are necessary conditions for a grants policy consistent with the continuing member vitality essential to a real federalism. They are not sufficient conditions. There must also be funds available to be distributed.

The public welcomes revenue distributions and curses taxes. Legislators therefore find more of the voter appeal they cultivate in the former than in the latter. It can plausibly be argued that a parliament empowered to impose taxes but not to direct spending will be reluctant to exert its power, with the result of drying up the pool of funds from which to make grants.

One reasonably positive assurance that there will indeed be money in the Canadian Equalization Fund flows from assigning to it the net proceeds of duties on imports. This compensates for the one exclusion from provincial taxing power, otherwise on the same plane as that of parliament. Of perhaps more significance, it tends to correct for the differential effect on provinces' economies arising from customs duties. Their desired and realized incidence by and large favours firms and products in proportion to the degree of the provinces' industrialization. That corresponds closely to their relative wealth. The protection duties afford is a charge on the entire Canadian market including buyers in the have-not provinces. In recapturing the net proceeds for distribution by the council, the proposal allows the continuation of a protective policy but tells against a duplication for the favoured provinces of its benefits, once by enlarging their own taxable resources and again by leaving the proceeds to be federally used to their advantage on the same basis as those where the net result of the policy is detrimental. The recurring international parleys looking to lowering tariff barriers may eventually free trade more than they have so far with a resultant shrinkage in Equalization Fund receipts from this source, but significant reduction seems far off and total elimination quite unlikely.

Section 87 of the Australian constitution is something of a precedent for this particular assignment, with its provision that three-fourths of the 'net revenue of the Commonwealth from duties of customs and of excise' should for the first ten years after the commonwealth's establishment be set aside for the states.

The net proceeds of import duties are a minor fraction of federal revenues. They are considerably less in amount than current transfer payments to other governments. For the Equalization Fund to be able to make grants of anything like the present magnitude they would need to be supplemented. Not that that present level is divinely ordained. Elimination of bureaucratic clutter through termination particularly of conditional grant programs could reduce associated administrative costs; but these tend to be only upwardly mobile so that net resources available for grant would probably be no more than marginally increased thereby.

The best prospect for a benignant readjustment of aggregate grant levels inheres in the difference between the standards historically applied and the constitutionally mandated concern with the provision 'of government services at a level worthy of Canadian life.' The latter implicates social and economic considerations. In this it contrasts with what has gone before, where political considerations dominate. All subventions have doubtless responded to a demand by some segment of the population, otherwise they would not have been enacted. But it is not clear that all would be seen to be supportive of 'government services' contributing to achieve 'a level worthy of Canadian life.' Provinces, it has been intimated, have been pressured into participation in grant programs which or at times which they would not have chosen voluntarily. That suggests that some electoral considerations persuasive at the federal level are not uniformly so in the provinces. The Equalization Council, with its carefully safeguarded insensitivity to them, might quite conceivably believe that an informed distribution of a total pool smaller because of the scrapping of certain programs could do more for relieving provincial disparities.

Naturally that is speculative. The council might just as possibly feel that the present total provision is about right or is inadequate. The point is only to avoid the trap of equating the present with the proper sum and asking what the likelihood is that that sum will be available under the arrangement proposed. Something besides the import duties will surely be needed. Prediction that parliament's loss of direction over spending may lessen its disposition to tax seems reasonable but, with no showing that the existing scale of transfer payments cannot be reduced at all without prejudice to underprivileged provinces, the prospect of some shrinkage is acceptable.

Altogether aside from import duties, a substantial excess of federal revenues over the outlays needed to maintain the federal establishment and perform the limited range of functions proposed to be left the central government is safely predictable. There will be some contribution from miscellaneous services – fines, royalties, fees, sale of assets. Their contribution while not trivial has been and may be expected to be modest in comparison with that made by taxes. Everything which swells the mass that may be drawn on only pursuant to parliamentary authorization thereby enters indistinguishably into the makeup of the surplus available to council requisition. Those other casual items will continue to add to the pool. But taxes must be looked to as the major component.

Were raising enough money to pay its household accounts the prime determinant of the tax structure, that would not be so. But the principal forces shaping fiscal policy have long been those associated with its use as an instrument for management of the economy. The diffuse unhappiness of taxpayers weighs less heavily in the legislative balance, especially where indirect taxes are concerned, than articulate demands marshalled in support of oblique market interventions or wealth-redistributive programs. These, it is foreseeable, will continue and will lose none of their effectiveness. Moreover, as long as the belief remains that business activity is significantly stimulated or dampened by fiscal measures with repercussions on inflation and unemployment, that consideration will eclipse the expenses involved in running the government as a tax policy thermostat. The proposed draft aims at enlarging rather than diminishing the central government's role as a regulator of the general level of economy. These considerations combine to support the conclusion that there will continue to be a surplus of federal revenues over federal needs despite parliament's inability to control its use. With that surplus, uncertain in amount but virtually certain to exist, added to the net proceeds of the import duties to which it is specifically entitled, the council will not be left allocating a derisory pittance. Should that, contrary to all reasonable expectation, prove to be the case, it might be necessary to look to the German solution but, because that would mean such a wholesale repatterning of the total constitutional structure, only as a last resort.

Unless there is really something at its disposal, the Equalization Fund will have a shadow discretion without the substance, whatever may appear on the federal income and expense statement. An abstract right to possession without provision for entry and ouster would mean little. One potential for parliament's extension of control into fields withheld from it would indeed be eliminated just by the denial of spending authority. Yet no benefits would accrue to the provinces if the result was simply to establish and enlarge a frozen account. The existence of such an overhanging reserve could even be a strong incentive to manoeuvre its release by extra-constitutional agreements with famished provinces. The circumvention of the states' rights to surplus, given by section 94 of the Australian constitution, through the artifice of labelling it a reserve is a cautionary illustration of the easy circumvention of declared rights left to parliamentary implementation. Instructed by that experience, the draft contains particulars for effectuating the transmission of revenues into the fund.

An annual cycle is made the norm for transfers both by the federal treasury to the fund and by the council of the provincial shares. Except as expressly authorized, the fund will be annually replenished and annually cleared without the hazard of accumulation as happened in Australia.

It is not required that the relevant year for requisitioning and that for grant allocation coincide. Nor, as to either the portion attributable to federal surplus or allocation, is the Council directed what year, calendar or fiscal, it shall use. The part representing the net proceeds of customs duties, being a non-discretionary item, is tied to the federal fiscal year for reasons of accounting convenience. Calculations of the surplus above

federal needs and the current relative insufficiency of provincial resources can be complex, calling for leeway in the selection of an appropriate and perhaps different year. That is best left to the council. Indeed as to
them it may take action at shorter intervals but must act at least annually.
This permits a prompt and flexible response to unforeseen events without
exposure of the grant program to dawdling or to deliberate stultification.

Transfer of the net proceeds of customs duties is made a regularly
recurring constitutional obligation of federal revenue officials. The claim
to surplus is activated by council requisition. Once that is communicated
to those officials, compliance with it too is an imperative obligation. Except
for exercise by the competent tribunal of the function of constitutional
interpretation, it is for the council to decide as well the size of the requisition as the timing within the year of requisitions and grants, a decision
which with that exception both federal and provincial governments must
accept.

The standard pattern contemplates that the net proceeds of customs
duties must and that ordinarily the ascertained surplus will each year be
cleared into the Equalization Fund and the whole amount, after deduct-
ing the council's operating costs, be cleared out of it by grants to provinces.
A departure from that usual course may, on occasion, be advisable.

For instance, in prosperous years even the needier provinces may be
able to meet substantially the cost of current operations although in the
long run change in the business cycle is a virtual certainty. A program for
replacing obsolescent or providing improved plant and equipment,
necessitating lumpy capital outlays, but generating an ampler stream of
government service over time, might be the provincially preferred way of
progress towards the level of performance posited. These as well as other
contingencies may call for accumulations which a mandatory annual
clearance would preclude. Authorizing the council to direct a holding in
reserve with respect to the surplus portion enables it to adjust the flow of
grants according to temporal variations in the demand for them.

A consideration of a quite different order further supports the council's
power to postpone requisitions in favor of the creation of a reserve. If
parliament, using fiscal policy as an instrument for regulating the general
level of the economy, sees fit to increase taxes with a view to reducing the
money in circulation to combat inflation, that purpose might measurably
be frustrated were it required to turn all the added proceeds over to the
provinces to be spent by them. To the extent that their spending created a
demand for resources otherwise unused for want of purchasing power,
which could be the case in some local markets, the impact on such an
anaemic demand-supply relation might not be prejudicial to federal policy. Nevertheless a considerable part of the grants would probably be used

to compete for commonly demanded goods and services as to which inflationary pressures were being experienced. Unless the council were allowed to annex program conditions to grants, a power which should be denied it for much the same reasons as have made its historic exercise by central governments dangerous, the contemporaneous addition to provincial purchasing power would work at cross purposes with the federal effort to damp down an overheated economy. The principle of fair shares to the less well-endowed provinces would not be furthered by aggravating a state of economic affairs injurious to all, to them as well as to their wealthier sisters.

The federal treasury would be accountable to the council for what was held as a reserve in amounts and at times determinable by the council. It might receive a customary management fee as a proper council expense. The reserve would not be subject to nor would it require appropriation by parliament.

Response to wartime or equivalent emergency demands was mentioned earlier as the sole legitimate use of federal revenue besides the paying for the execution of the assigned federal functions and the easing of provincial inequality. Even that would not alter the status of the federal government as a mere custodian of the excess. Payments associated with the execution of federal functions would of course swell enormously and any excess of federal revenues coming to the fund would decrease correspondingly, perhaps disappear altogether. If, as might well be, that proved insufficient, the accumulated reserve might indeed have to be freed for federal use, a contingency for which the draft provides.

It would not become so automatically nor at the discretion of parliament nor indeed at the discretion of the Equalization Council. The governing provision is section ( ).[15] It recognizes an exception to the council's right of direction of excess revenue. The operative condition is the unanimous concurrence of the provinces. This would fall to be signified by their governments by statutes expressing their consent or delegating authority to do so. Council members could not act by express or implied delegation even by unanimous consent since their members 'shall not act under or for any particular government.'

The experience of both Canada and Australia in world war II justifies the faith that unanimous concurrence can be had when the public feels there is a real threat. But only then. Concurrence might be conditioned as to time or otherwise, being effective only insofar as there was unanimity. Letting the provinces lift the otherwise applicable constitutional restrictions on federal spending permits a release of resources to parliament's

15 Supra, at 55.

control in a genuine crisis without risking the sorry fate of the reserve called for by the Australian constitution. The provision for exemption by the provinces' concurrence is not limited to current annual income. If that condition is satisfied, their power to withdraw from council direction for federal use applies equally to anything accumulated as a reserve by virtue of prior council action.

The foregoing deals with revenues to be held subject to current or postponed requisition. The council's discretion about that needs to be complemented by a discretion as to amounts turned over to the fund pursuant to requisition.

In general, allocations to the provinces are to be made annually on a scale matching the requisitions. There is one qualification. The council may establish a contingency reserve for disasters.

This is the only departure from the requirement that whatever amount the council decides should go to a province must be paid over 'without condition.' Its competence as a supreme court of welfare economics for appraising the provinces' over-all relative possession of resources to provide services at a level worthy of Canadian life does not extend to the detail of settling priorities among the competing demands on the provinces' limited resources. That is a matter peculiarly for determination by the people of the province themselves acting through their elected representatives. The matter might be left there if all provincial operations could be periodically budgeted for with assurance that no major disturbances from outside would create exceptional demands. That cannot be. Prairie droughts, coastal oil spills, are certain to occur although their incidence is uncertain. Provision must be made for fortuitous events aggravating the strain on already fully assigned resources. While the council, called on to make allocations 'at least annually' may make them oftener, that would involve a fresh consideration of the relative entitlement of all claimant provinces, a proceeding not expeditious enough for instant response to a crisis situation in only one or two provinces. Unanimous concurrence of the provinces in recognition of a national crisis cannot be relied on for a situation where there is no animating threat to a common interest. Nor would it be well to open up any loophole for parliament to assume direction of what a province should spend. That can more safely be done by a body which, had the disaster been foreseeable, would have taken it into account in determining the adequacy of provincial resources to provide services made necessary by reason of its occurrence. It can be thought of as revising a grant to the level it would have attained had the disaster been forecast. To that limited extent and for that limited purpose, the council would be able to direct the end to which a grant could be put.

By way of summary, the thesis maintained is that it is chiefly central control of spending that has undermined the whole structure of federalism. It must be harnessed to its proper purposes – execution of assigned federal functions, contingent provisions for crises, finally spreading participation in the fruits of association without impinging on the policy preferences of provinces. The federal government would be and it should be shorn of funds for implementing asserted 'national policies' on other matters. The very assertion is a usurpation when it extends beyond its assigned constitutional competence.

To keep it within proper bounds and at the same time aid the less fortunate partners to share in the material benefits arising from association, the system defects that have regularly plagued grant programs – programme-linked distributions, determination by federal political authorities, fixed or formula entitlements – must disappear. Awards must be made by a qualified independent body analogous in the discipline of welfare economics to a court of law, exercising informed discretion toward the stated end of alleviating disparities.

I am aware that what is here proposed will be vigorously resisted by some elected representatives but even more by the extensive and in many ways admirable bureaucracies that have evolved for the administration of the existing scheme of things. Dismantling them will not be easy. It must be slowly and carefully worked out. I may indeed be chimerical in thinking opposition to it by those in place can be overcome. Without it, however, we are doomed to see disappear all hope of dispersed control of policy priorities and, with that gone, of a long continuance of a common country.

Canadian University Paperbooks
of related interest

CPSIA information can be obtained
at www.ICGtesting.com
Printed in the USA
LVOW08s1016090417

530147LV00001B/4/P

9 780802 063991